Poor Pearl, Poor Girl!

Publications of the American Folklore Society

MEMOIR SERIES

Wm. Hugh Jansen, General Editor

Volume 58   1973

POOR PEARL, POOR GIRL!

The Murdered-Girl Stereotype in Ballad and Newspaper

ANNE B. COHEN

PUBLISHED FOR THE AMERICAN FOLKLORE SOCIETY BY
THE UNIVERSITY OF TEXAS PRESS, AUSTIN AND LONDON

Library of Congress Cataloging in Publication Data

Cohen, Anne B   1937–
  Poor Pearl, poor girl!

  (Publications of the American Folklore Society.
Memoir series, v. 58)
  Bibliography: p.
  1. Folk literature, American—History and criticism.
2. Bryan, Pearl, d. 1896.   3. American ballads
and songs—History and criticism.   I. Title.
II. Series: American Folklore Society. Memoirs,
v. 58.
PS461.B7C6   810'.9'351   73-7919
ISBN 0-292-76409-X

Composition by G&S Typesetters, Austin
Printing by The University of Texas Printing Division, Austin
Binding by Universal Bookbindery, Inc., San Antonio

TO NORM

CONTENTS

ILLUSTRATIONS

ACKNOWLEDGMENTS

It is a pleasure to express my indebtedness to the following people: D. K. Wilgus for directing the master's thesis on which this study is based; Robert A. Georges for the initial advice and encouragement to rewrite the thesis as a book; Marina Bokelman, Joseph Hickerson, and Judith McCulloh for out-of-the-way texts; and my husband, Norm, for discographical data, uncompromising criticism, and unflagging moral support.

Poor Pearl, Poor Girl!

1. INTRODUCTION

WEIRD
Even to Fascination
The Story of the Murder of Pearl Bryan
Details of the Tragedy Once
More Recalled

On February 1, 1896, a boy discovered the headless body of a woman in a farmer's field not far from Fort Thomas, Kentucky. On February 2 the coroner's report revealed that the victim had been five months pregnant. It was presumed that the father of the baby, whoever he was, was the murderer of the girl. By February 5 the body was identified as that of Pearl Bryan, twenty-three-year-old daughter of a prosperous farmer in Greencastle, Indiana. One day later one of her beaux, Scott Jackson, then a dental student in Cincinnati, was arrested and charged with her murder. Jackson's roommate, Alonzo Walling, was subsequently arrested on the same charge. The successful argument of the prosecution in the trials of the two men was that they had attempted an abortion on Pearl and that when this failed they murdered her by decapitation. The two men were hanged on the same gallows March 20, 1897, protesting their innocence to the last. Pearl Bryan's head was never found.

In capsule form, this is the series of events which for a year monopolized the front pages and Sunday supplements of newspapers in Indiana, Ohio, and Kentucky, and which inspired at least six ballads that had some currency in folk tradition.

The present study attempts to show that the ballads based on the Pearl Bryan case are examples of "formulaic" composition, if the term "formula" is given a broader sense than is usually granted it. The term "formula" as used by scholars of the epic, such as Albert Lord and C. M. Bowra,[1] refers only to set sequences (or patterns for sequences) of words. The term "theme" is used to refer to such recurring items as battle scenes, the sending and receiving of messages, feasts, descriptions of clothes, and so on. I find it convenient to have one expression covering both types of recurring elements and therefore use the term "formula" to include set sequences of words, set scenes, set sequences of action, and set characters. Further, for the purposes pursued in this book, there is no assumption about whether the formulae considered are oral in origin.

A comparison of newspaper and ballad accounts of the crime shows that some of the formulae found in the Pearl Bryan ballads are not the property of balladry alone, but, rather, are shared by nineteenth-century journalism.[2] Both media tell the story from the same moral stance, express the same interpretation of character, and are interested in the same details. Both tend to distort facts to accommodate a shared pattern of storytelling. The shared pattern consists basically of a plot formula that has an attendant company of other formulae, such as stereotyped scenes, stereotyped actors, and stereotyped phrases.

This plot formula, a popular one in white American balladry, has been noted before[3] and is usually called the "murdered-girl"

[1] See, for example, C. M. Bowra, *Heroic Poetry*, and Albert Lord, *The Singer of Tales*.

[2] Further study will probably find these formulae occurring also in other forms of nineteenth-century popular literature, such as the melodrama and the dime novel.

[3] E.g., Henry M. Belden, "Balladry in America," *Journal of American*

story. Presumably, this plot formula is a "construct" or "archetype" of some kind existing in the minds of those people who write newspaper stories and those people who compose ballads, such that it influences, if not their perception of events, at least their framing of these events into narratives. (I assume further that these formulae are shared also by large numbers of the reading and listening public who accept and preserve these narratives.) The result of this formulaic filter, through which information passes, is that stories tend to be altered progressively toward greater and greater similarity to the model. Through time, distinguishing features that one might expect to be remembered because of their striking character are actually blurred and lost if they conflict with the model. Similarly, features that originally had no part in a story will be drawn to it if they belong to the formula influencing that story.

It is exactly this process which we see occurring, over a seventy-year time span, in the Pearl Bryan ballads. To a lesser extent one can see it in newspaper accounts over the thirteen-month period in which this story was prominently featured.

The influence of the formula or model is felt not only in the progressively greater resemblance of the story to the model. Indeed, there is a constant tension between "fact" and "formula" from the very beginning, and the story does not develop linearly toward the model. Disturbing influences occur, and "facts" obtrude rudely at times. For instance, it will be argued that Walling was perceived as a secondary figure because the model murdered-girl story had no place for him. Yet, just before Walling's execution Governor Bradley of Kentucky issued a statement reviewing his reasons for refusing clemency to Walling; this action had enough effect on public opinion to restore Wall-

---

Folklore 25 (1912): 10; J. H. Combs, *Folk-Songs of the Southern United States,* p. 55; G. Malcolm Laws, Jr., *Native American Balladry,* p. 22; Louise Pound, *American Ballads and Songs,* p. 22.

ing for a time to the position of importance, and of guilt, which he had held briefly at the conclusion of his trial.

More speculatively, I would suggest that certain stereotyped characters and situations appearing in nineteenth-century American popular literature reflect contemporary social ideas. Stock characters of folksong and popular literature, such as the wily city seducer and the trusting country maid, may represent a popular mode of perceiving the social order in terms of the wholesome but simple (in both senses) country pitted against the clever but unscrupulous city. Moreover, in these stereotypes the "good," morally approved characters are by and large passive sufferers; the villains are active "doers." This theme of the passive sufferings of a "good" character contrasted with the energetic activity of the "bad" person can be traced through the music of the upper South from the nineteenth-century "Little Blossom," "Henry Green," and "Just Plain Folks" through the modern country western "See the Big Man Cry," "Mama," and "Devil Woman."

These formulae may reflect one continuing mode of perception (though certainly not the only one) of the moral value of social roles. A constant exposure to models of "goodness," whose most notable characteristic is passive endurance, may be one among many influences working against social change.[4] Certainly it is

[4] If we assume for the moment that there is a widespread behavior model in some communities that represents ordinary, decent people as essentially passive in their response to events, trusting Providence to direct the course of their lives, we may be able to explain a variety of social consequences. For example, a provocative study by John H. Sims and Duane D. Bauman, "The Tornado Threat: Coping Styles of the North and South," *Science* 176 (30 June 1972), 1386–1392, explores the possibility that psychological responses may account for the disproportionately high fatality rate from tornadoes in the South compared to other sections of the country. Their conclusion, based on sentence-completion tests given to respondents in tornado-prone areas of Alabama and Illinois, is essentially that the Southerner's attitude toward disaster is passive and fatalistic, lead-

not inconsistent with the "folk conservatism" often noted by
field workers and may be a hypothesis that is worth future ex-
ploration.

------

ing him to do little to protect himself or others, while the Northerner
actively uses community resources to protect himself and aid his neighbors.
For example, in completing the sentence "The survivors of a tornado . . . ,"
the Illinoisans gave a high percentage of answers of the sort ". . . need to
be helped"; the Alabamans were more prone to express their sympathy in
feeling than in action, in such responses as ". . . feel terrible."

Although responses of Alabamans to tornadoes may seem a far cry from
the presentation of character in folk songs, I submit that there is in both
cases a similar perception of appropriate behavior for good people in the
face of danger: they may pray, weep, and implore, but then they resign
themselves to fate. It would be inconceivable for the American murdered-
girl heroine to take action to save herself, as does the heroine of the
European ballad "Lady Isabel and the Elf Knight" (Number 4 in Francis
James Child's *The English and Scottish Popular Ballads*). Lady Isabel is,
like the American murdered-girl heroine, lured to a lonely spot with
promises of marriage, only to find herself in the arms of a murderer; unlike
Pearl Bryan, Pretty Polly, Omie Wise, and Florella, however, the resourceful Lady Isabel turns the tables on her would-be assassin and does him in
most adroitly.

2. THE NEWSPAPERS

Lured from Her Peaceful Country Home
To Her Death in the Dark Mazes of
a Great City—The Crime of
the Century

The newspapers of the larger cities in Ohio, Indiana, and Kentucky devoted considerable space to the Pearl Bryan murder over the thirteen-month period from the day her headless corpse was found to the day her convicted murderers were hanged. At a time when regionalism was more pronounced than it is today, the citizens of these states appear to have had a "personal" interest in the case. It was Cincinnati, Ohio, to which Pearl had come for an abortion, and where her two murderers attended dental school. Alonzo Walling, one of the murderers, was a native of Hamilton, Ohio. Pearl, as well as her slayer, Scott Jackson, came from Greencastle, Indiana. Her body was found in Fort Thomas, Kentucky, and it was in Kentucky where the two men were tried and executed.

The literally hundreds of column inches devoted to the case by the newspapers provide ample data for the thesis of this study—that newspaper and ballad accounts framed events in the same narrative formulae. At the same time, however, the papers were reporting news and have been used as sources of fact as well as of formula.

A note may be in order about the use of newspaper accounts as sources both for factual reporting and for distortion toward models or stereotypes. It may well be asked: how does one tell the difference between a factual statement and one that is "adjusted" by the influence of stereotypes? I used the following guidelines to distinguish "fact" from "formula":

First, comparison of different news accounts. If an incident or detail is reported independently in two or more newspapers, I have assumed it more likely to have happened than if it was reported in one only.

Second, comparison of different accounts of the same events at different times. If the story, or interpretation, changes even when the evidence has not, distortion toward a model may have taken place. This is particularly evident in summaries of the crime given shortly after the trials and then again a year later, after the hanging of the convicted men.

Third, attention to what incidents are selected for inclusion in résumés of the case. This selection presumably indicates what was considered significant. If these résumés tend to resemble a model murdered-girl plot, it is assumed that the model may have influenced perception of what was important in the case.

Fourth, the use of independent evidence. One of the most important is the daily transcript of the court proceedings during Jackson's trial, given in the Cincinnati *Enquirer*. The same evidence, for the most part, was used in the trials of both Jackson and Walling. Thus, it is possible to compare many newspaper accounts with the evidence on which they were based.

Finally, there is a tendency in all the newspaper accounts to describe events in terms that reflect personal judgments or to describe things that reporters could not have known. For example, if a newspaper story says an "icy chill ran down Scott Jackson's spine as he sees [sic] a photo of the headless body,"[1] it is assumed that the reporter was romancing. Given the situation, the reporter had no way of ascertaining whether anything had run down Jackson's spine. Examples of the use of terms reflecting private judgments include "poor Pearl," "an estimable lady," "the inhuman fiends Jackson and Walling," and "a bright-faced country boy was gayly tripping across field and meadow."

In some cases the subjective terms seem somewhat at variance with the events described. A rather grim speech by Pearl's father, for example, was quoted in a context abounding with affliction, woe, and pathos.[2] In such cases as these it has been assumed that the apparently inappropriate terms are expressions of What-Ought-To-Be for the purposes of a story formula and that, while the newspapers are constrained somewhat by their function as newspapers to report what happens, the influence of stereotypes finds expression in the free use of these subjective terms.

Now that the reader is warned of my approach and methods, we may proceed to an examination of the newspaper accounts themselves.

On February 2, 1896, newspaper readers in Ohio, Indiana, and Kentucky received their first notice of what was to become "The Crime of the Century." Newspapers in major cities reported that a small boy had discovered the body of a headless woman in an unused field owned by John Lock, a farmer near Fort Thomas. The body was removed to Newport, where the coroner's initial examination led him to say that the victim had not been raped, but that she "had been a mother." The victim

---

[1] *Evening Post* (Louisville), April 29, 1896.
[2] This speech is given below (*Enquirer* [Cincinnati], February 7, 1896).

was described by the Cincinnati *Enquirer* as "a woman of the town," "of not more than middle age," whose clothing was "of the cheapest description."[3] Cleveland's *Plain Dealer* reported that she was probably "an abandoned woman from Cincinnati."[4] Her dress was of the sort that "a woman of the lower class would wear indoors, and, covered with a cloak, on the street."[5] It was assumed by both police and newspapers that the woman was of low class and ill repute because her body was found near a fort and because she was not a virgin.

A single fact, announced the next day, changed the picture drawn of the victim: the coroner's report revealed that the woman had been pregnant. At once, from an abandoned woman of not more than middle age, she became "a young and trusting girl, whose only offense was having loved too well."[6] Moreover, it was now certain that "she was murdered by the man, or at the instigation of the man responsible for her shame."[7]

Speaking from the official level, one of the doctors attending at the post-mortem was able to give a rather detailed account of the crime, remarkable considering that he had only a pregnant corpse as evidence:

I am satisfied that the girl was not outraged. The man had a reason to kill her, and the result of the post mortem showed it. I judge that it was premeditated and cold-blooded murder. The girl, in my opinion, was from the country and was comparatively innocent. She was brought to Cincinnati to submit to a criminal operation. Once here she was taken to Fort Thomas and murdered. Her head was taken away, horrible as it may seem, merely to prevent the identification of her body. Yes, it would be very easy for a man to cut a woman's head off with

[3] *Enquirer* (Cincinnati), February 2, 1896.
[4] *Plain Dealer* (Cleveland), February 2, 1896.
[5] *Enquirer* (Cincinnati), February 2, 1896.
[6] Ibid., February 4, 1896.
[7] Ibid.

a knife, even if he had no knowledge of anatomy. I could cut off a woman's head with a small penknife and it wouldn't take long to do it.[8]

These statements suggest that nineteenth-century Cincinnati needed no more than a pregnant female corpse to prove to it that the entire American Tragedy, so often repeated in folksong, had again run its course.

This transformation from abandoned city woman to trusting country maid was only the first in a series of adjustments in the story as it appeared from day to day in the newspapers. As time passed, the story of Pearl Bryan's murder took on the contours of the murdered-girl plot found in such popular folksongs as "Fair Florella," "Pretty Polly," "Knoxville Girl," "Banks of the Ohio," "Omie Wise," and "Rose Connoley." Not only were events adjusted to conform to formula, but the individuals involved were also perceived as stereotypes; they were stock characters in a melodrama acting out a well-known plot.

Pearl's family, apparently tough and vengeful, were interpreted as passive, careworn, and weary, even while actions were reported of them that did not conform to this interpretation. Consider the following extract from a news story:

The Aged Father of the Murdered Girl Talks to a Reporter

"And did they find the head?" asked the old man through his tears. He was told that at that time the head had not been found. "Oh, I hope they will [find it]. We don't want to have it said above her grave: Here lies the body of a headless woman. That would only serve to perpetuate our bitter recollections. But," and the old man straightened up in his chair, and, raising his hand toward heaven, said in a voice that was chilling in its tones, "Terrible as her fate was, and much as we deplore it, we would rather endure the torture of a daughter lured to ruin by a villain

[8] Ibid.

than the infamy of a son who stands charged with such a crime."

As he spoke the words a hush fell upon the room. The mother bowed her head and sobbed, and men and women in the room cried like children. It was a scene that would touch the hardest heart.[9]

Taken out of their sentimental context, the ideas expressed by Mr. Bryan are rather tough ones: Pearl's head must be found in order to avoid public comment; and it is better to have a dead daughter than a guilty son.

Some of Pearl's family apparently formed part of an unsuccessful lynching party prior to Jackson's trial.[10] Pearl's parents and one or more siblings sat through every day of the trials of both Jackson and Walling and did so without breaking down, although spectators in the courtroom and members of the jury wept openly at some of the more pathetic descriptions of Pearl's experience and at some of the gruesome artifacts produced by the prosecution.[11] Occasionally, a member of the Bryan family made an angry remark in the courtroom. For example, when a witness testified that he saw Jackson, Walling, and Pearl eating at a family restaurant, Mrs. Bryan cried out, "Thank God they took her to one decent place after dragging her around in the [blur] all the rest of the time!"[12] The family actively assisted the prosecution, and Mr. Bryan sat throughout both trials at the table of the prosecution. The active and morbid interest of the Bryans in the case is shown by their presentation of a rather grisly reward to a man instrumental in tracking down the murderers: "Shoemaker Poock, of Newport, who was the first to suggest that Pearl Bryan's shoes, which led to her identification

[9] Ibid., February 7, 1896.

[10] Ibid., March 19, 1896.

[11] *Evening Post* (Louisville), April 29, 1896; *Enquirer* (Cincinnati), April 23, 24, 26, 1896.

[12] *Daily Banner Times* (Greencastle), June 6, 1896.

and the arrest of the suspected murderers, might form an important clew, has been presented with the identical pair of shoes by the girl's parents."[13]

Twice, members of the Bryan family visited the spot where Pearl's remains were found, examined the blood-stained ground, and quizzed the owner of the land about details of the discovery of the body.[14] Fred Bryan twice and his sister once confronted Scott Jackson in prison, and Fred apparently threatened Jackson.[15] After the execution Mr. Bryan and Fred Bryan expressed their satisfaction and their "kindly feelings" toward Governor Bradley for refusing respite to Walling.[16]

Despite this evidence that Pearl's family kept a stiff upper lip and that much of their feeling found expression in anger, there was a strong tendency to portray them as passively grief-stricken, like the careworn parents and weeping sisters of vulgar balladry. It is noteworthy perhaps that neither of Pearl's two brothers was described alone with adjectives emanating pathos attached to him. Only when mentioned as part of the "heart-broken family" could a brother claim these adjectives. The expressions "utterly heartbroken," "sorrowing," "grief-stricken," "stunned," and "full of pathos" were used to refer only to the family as a whole or to the father, mother, and sister individually. In addition, Mr. and Mrs. Bryan collected the adjectives "silver-haired," "grey-haired," and "aged."

I think it likely that this selective application of epithets is again a matter of formulaic description. Young men in the prime of life are not appropriately described in terms of passive suffer-

[13] *Enquirer* (Cincinnati), February 21, 1896.

[14] *Star-Press* (Greencastle), February 15 and March 14, 1896; *Enquirer* (Cincinnati), undated clipping from the newspaper morgue.

[15] *Star-Press* (Greencastle), February 15, 1896; *Evening Post* (Louisville), February 8, 1896; *Greencastle Democrat* (Greencastle), February 15, 1896.

[16] *Enquirer* (Cincinnati), March 21, 1897.

ing, at least not in the murdered-girl formula. There are two situation formulae in American popular literature that do feature lachrymose young men: (1) the criminal brought to justice, and (2) the lad unfortunate in love. (The criminal-brought-to-justice formula will be described in Chapter 3.) Since the Bryan boys could not be fitted into either of these categories there were no standard epithets lying to hand for the reporters grinding out the daily installments of the Crime of the Century. We will see later that the criminal-brought-to-justice formula did affect accounts centering on the last days of the convicted men, Jackson and Walling.

For the afflicted parents, however, these prefabricated descriptive patterns appear abundantly. "Aged," for example, almost invariably accompanied the word "parent." This was also true when the expression was used to describe the mothers of Jackson and Walling. In fact, the characterizations of the three mothers were almost indistinguishable. All were "aged," "silver-haired," "bowed down with grief," and prematurely old from sorrow. Compare the following descriptions given of the three women:

Mrs. Bryan is a motherly-looking woman of 60, and she was dressed yesterday in deep mourning. . . . [Her] voice was quavering with nervousness and emotion, as well as with age.[17]

Mrs. Jackson is a most estimable lady . . . A milder looking, sweeter-faced woman than she never lived. Her hair, iron-gray before her greatest trouble, now as white as snow, is brushed evenly back from a broad intellectual looking forehead. . . . but for the disgrace and trouble brought upon her by her son, . . . [she] might have lived to a ripe old age.[18]

No matter how dark may grow the clouds which are fast en-

[17] Ibid., April 24, 1896.
[18] *Evening Post* (Louisville), March 20, 1897.

veloping Scott Jackson, one heart at least will be true to him—
that of his aged mother. In striking contrast to the terrible crime
of which he is suspected is the pure, unselfish and confiding love
of that mother.[19]

. . . the broken-hearted mother of Alonzo Walling . . . the grey-
haired mother, whose cup of sorrow has been well-nigh filled
to overflowing.[20]

[Mrs. Walling] sat with an air of resignation, apparently oblivi-
ous to her surroundings. . . . The prisoner hurried forward and
imprinted a kiss on his aged mother's quivering lips. The action
seemed to awaken sympathy for both, and several ladies in the
audience wept at the sight.[21]

As she [Mrs. Walling] was going she stopped and said something to him in a low tone, pressing her motherly face against
the iron bars. There were tears in her eyes and her lips
trembled.[22]

The following extract suggests that when there were no signs
of sorrowing motherhood, the reporter himself supplied them:

At no time did the poor mother [Mrs. Jackson] give vent to an
audible sound, but retained herself composedly.

Close scrutiny, however, showed that there was much pent-
up emotion, which might break out at any time. Her outward
appearance was no indication of her inward feelings.[23]

The character of Pearl Bryan was as fixed in popular accounts
as that of the aged parents and sorrowing families. Although
there was evidence that she had bestowed her favors on more
than one man and that she was capable (in 1896!) of going off

19 *Enquirer* (Cincinnati), February 6, 1896.
20 Ibid., March 21, 1897.
21 Ibid., June 9, 1896.
22 Ibid., March 6, 1897.
23 *Evening Post* (Louisville), May 2, 1896.

by herself to Cincinnati to have an abortion, she was "poor innocent Pearl" to the public. She was portrayed as a naive and confiding girl, led astray by a sophisticated villain who preferred murdering her to marrying her: "Jackson was determined to be rid of the trusting country girl he ruined."[24]

Pearl's family received sympathetic letters from all parts of the country: "One letter that is especially prized by the sorrowing family was written by Prof. Lyon, now of Boston, who was formerly Miss Bryan's high school instructor. It bears testimony to her high standing as a pupil, no less than her spotless purity of character."[25] At Pearl's funeral the minister "paid a high tribute to the character of the departed daughter, her confiding, trustful nature, and marked amiability of spirit."[26]

The crime against Pearl was described as "cruel betrayal," and stern punishment was demanded for those "preying upon the innocent and unsophisticated."[27] A number of sermons were preached in 1896 and 1897 drawing lessons from Pearl Bryan's fate. Although sometimes referred to as "erring," Pearl was more often described in such language as "the poor weak victim of a man's rapacious lust and fiendish brutality."[28]

That the public wanted to believe in Pearl's purity is shown in a story told in the Greencastle *Star-Press*. A rumor was circulating in Greencastle that, while Jackson was working in a local dentist's office, Pearl complained to him of a toothache. Jackson told her to come to the office, knowing that Dr. Gillespie, the dentist, would be away. He then reputedly operated on Pearl, using cocaine to render her unconscious. The paper reports:

[24] Ibid., February 8, 1896.

[25] *Enquirer* (Cincinnati), February 29, 1896.

[26] Ibid., March 28, 1896.

[27] *Star-Press* (Greencastle), February 15, 1896.

[28] Sermon preached by Rev. D. McKinley at the Reformed Presbyterian Church in Cincinnati, reported in the *Enquirer* (Cincinnati), February 10, 1896.

Miss Bryan was in the office, in an unconscious condition, for almost two hours.

People here are of the opinion that it was there that Scott Jackson ruined the girl whom he is now alleged to have murdered. It is stated, on quite reliable authority, that this story will be told on the witness stand at the proper time.[29]

In fact, this story never was told on the witness stand, and Dr. Gillespie hastened to contradict it. He said that Jackson had the keys to his office only twice, and neither occasion was at a time when the rape was alleged to have taken place.[30]

Another popular belief was that after she reached Cincinnati Pearl decided not to have an abortion after all, or that she never intended to have an abortion, but came to the big city to try to persuade Jackson to marry her.[31]

The Cincinnati *Enquirer* told its readers that the story of Pearl's fate was "a simple tale" of an "innocent girl" who "loved too well." She was "charming and lovable," her parents' "pride and joy," and filled the parental home "with the sunshine of her presence."[32]

[29] *Star-Press* (Greencastle), March 14, 1896.

[30] The idea of unprofessional conduct in the dentist's office is widespread, and a traveling motif may have attached itself here to the Pearl Bryan story. The idea has certainly persisted in bawdy form. D. K. Wilgus has called to my attention two limericks in G. Legman, *The Limerick*:

No. 81   There was a young lady named Prentice
          Who had an affair with a dentist
          To make things easier
          He used anesthesia
          And diddled her, *non compos mentis.*

No. 102   There once was a dentist named Stone
          Who saw all his patients alone
          In a fit of depravity
          He filled the wrong cavity
          And my, how his practice has grown.

[31] *Enquirer* (Cincinnati), March 2, 1896; *Daily Banner Times* (Greencastle), April 27, 1896.

[32] *Enquirer* (Cincinnati), April 19, 1896.

A year later, summarizing the case, the *Enquirer* said:

*Lured from Her Peace-
ful Country Home*

---

*To Her Death in the Dark
Mazes of a Great
City—The Crime
of the Century*

This is the story of the greatest crime of the century. It is the story of a tragedy that had its inception in the whispered words and sweet caresses of love far away from the noise and smoke of the city in the quaint old country town of Greencastle, Ind.; a tragedy that ended for a beautiful, trusting girl amid the bleak hills of the Kentucky Highlands; a crime that was expiated yesterday by her betrayer and his friend upon the scaffold.[33]

Pearl's clothing as well as Pearl's character attracted sentiment commensurate with the role it played. When it was believed she was a prostitute, Pearl's dress was described as "lower class" and "of the cheapest description."[34] Later, when Pearl was established as a reputable girl of good family, the dress appeared in contexts of sentiment and respect:

*Heartrending Scene as the Dead Girl's Mother
Identified her Clothing*

. . . One by one the garments last worn by the dead girl were shown to the mother and as she identified each particular piece the scene was one to appall the stoutest heart. . . . With pathetic anguish she hung over the dead girl's dress. It had been worn by another daughter, Jennie, who died last June.[35]

[33] Ibid., March 21, 1897.
[34] Ibid., February 2, 1896.
[35] Ibid., February 6, 1896.

Mrs. Stanley [Pearl's sister] . . . came into the courtroom clad in deep mourning, and when she threw back her veil she revealed a countenance of extraordinary refinement and intelligence. . . . Her eyes filled with tears as she handled the clothing of the dead girl, and said, "I know this was my sister's dress, for I helped to make it."[36]

Surely a woman of extraordinary refinement and intelligence would not make dresses "of the cheapest description."

The characters of Scott Jackson and Alonzo Walling were also subject to newspaper interpretation. At first, while Jackson and Walling were merely under arrest and the police were busy gathering evidence, accounts of them varied. It was not yet entirely settled who was to be the principal murderer and who the assistant murderer, nor was it settled whether Scott Jackson or Will Wood, Pearl's cousin in Greencastle, was the betrayer of the girl.

In one account we are told, "Jackson speaks stolidly, but looks as if he would burst with remorse."[37] Another describes Jackson as follows: "Jackson was terribly excited and nervously clasped and unclasped his hands. His eyes roved from one end of the body to the other and he shook his head and sighed deeply. His face was terribly flushed, and he looked as though he might break down every second."[38] In the same story, it was said: "Walling was to all appearances the coolest man in the room. He gazed at the corpse without a shiver and looked around on the faces of those present."[39] This picture of the nervous, remorseful Jackson and the coolly unmoved Walling was to be completely reversed as the story crystallized into a standard form.

---

[36] *Star-Press* (Greencastle), April 25, 1896.
[37] *Evening Post* (Louisville), February 6, 1896.
[38] *Enquirer* (Cincinnati), February 9, 1896.
[39] Ibid.

The next day the same newspaper carried a description of Jackson as "cool and collected, and . . . the coldest blooded fellow ever locked up in jail."[40] Yet three days later the same paper reported:

> Yesterday was visitors' day at the jail, and Jailer Kushman had his hands full. Besides the hundreds who called to see other prisoners twice as many called to see Jackson and Walling. . . . The officers have taken to asking all the visitors whom they think did the killing, and every one so far has said "Walling." No matter who it is, man or woman, when asked for an opinion the reply is always "I think Walling did it, as Jackson does not look like he would do a thing like that."[41]

At the same time, both men were described as "stubborn, stolid and heartless,"[42] and Jackson was said to have had a "stolid, half stupid and always argumentative manner."[43]

Another interpretation of the characters of the two, one which in one form or another was to become the standard, was also advanced at this time. On February 9, the Cincinnati *Enquirer* carried the results of a phrenological examination of Jackson and Walling, made at police headquarters by a Dr. Hyndman. In sum, Jackson was described as "nervous," with "good, quick reasoning power . . . a bold, fearless, intense organization, with a perverted amativeness. . . . would mislead anyone to assist himself and has strong perceptive power . . . a good planner, and a fearless executioner." Walling's skull pronounced him "easily led in the direction of friendship," in whose cause "he would often do things which his better nature would revolt against. . . . His standard of morals is not of a high order, his perceptive powers are small, and if he would be influenced he

[40] Ibid., February 10, 1896.
[41] Ibid., February 13, 1896.
[42] *Star-Press* (Greencastle), February 15, 1896.
[43] *Plain Dealer* (Cleveland), February 7, 1896.

would have to be managed through his self-approbation. He is susceptible to flattery and would make a confidant of one who would flatter him in this manner."[44] Here the groundwork is laid for the interpretation of Jackson as the bold planner and executor of the murder, with Walling his easily directed assistant.

A few days later this interpretation was carried further in a story about the attempted hypnosis of Jackson and Walling. The police, in an attempt to gather more evidence in the case, decided to have the prisoners hypnotized, hoping they would reveal heretofore suppressed evidence. After an unsuccessful attempt on Jackson, the hypnotist, Dr. Schoemer, is reported to have said: "That man is a hypnotist if there ever was one, and if he has knowledge that he possesses that terrible power it may suggest a different theory than has yet been presented."[45]

The attempt to hypnotize Walling was also unsuccessful, although Dr. Schoemer felt that Walling was by nature a good subject. The newspaper account concluded with these words:

> No further attempt was made to draw Walling out. His last words were in the nature of confirmation of the doctor's opinion that Jackson could have exercised a momentous influence over Walling if he had tried, and which he might have done either consciously or unconsciously. In the opinion of Dr. Schoemer, Jackson's hypnotic suggestion might have armed Walling's hand with the fatal weapon, indicated and compelled the murder of poor Pearl Bryan and still Walling would have been totally unconscious of his dreadful deed not alone during its commission but also after its completion.[46]

The view that Walling was simply the docile instrument of Jackson's will became a very popular one. While in February and March of 1896 he was often described in such terms as "cold

44 *Enquirer* (Cincinnati), February 9, 1896.
45 Ibid., February 11, 1896.
46 Ibid., February 11, 1896.

and calculating,"[47] "stubborn, stolid, and heartless,"[48] and a "cold-blooded villain,"[49] a year later, at the time of his execution, he was described in the following words: "Alonzo Walling —the man whom Jackson worked as a tool";[50] "Jackson cared nothing for Walling but to use him as a tool";[51] "In temperament he is stolid and morose, with little force of character, which made him all the more pliant tool of Jackson."[52] A contemporary observer of the case, M. W. Pinkerton of Pinkerton & Company's United States Detective Agency, noted this popular interpretation of Walling's character, although he did not personally subscribe to it: "It was claimed that he was a weak man mentally, that he had no motive to commit the crime, and had been led, forced, into it, by the dominant will of Jackson."[53]

When Walling was not seen as Jackson's puppet, he was usually viewed as an accomplice rather than as a co-engineer of the crime. He was almost always described as, in some sense, less guilty than Jackson. Before Jackson's trial, which preceded Walling's, a rumor circulated that Walling would turn state's evidence, that Jackson would thereby be certain of conviction, and that Walling would get a light sentence.[54] Shortly before the execution many news stories contained reports that Governor Bradley would commute Walling's sentence[55] or that Jackson would confess and exonerate Walling[56] or that evidence

---

[47] *Daily Banner Times* (Greencastle), March 2, 1896.
[48] *Star-Press* (Greencastle), February 15, 1896.
[49] *Evening Post* (Louisville), February 10, 1896.
[50] Ibid., March 20, 1897.
[51] *Enquirer* (Cincinnati), March 21, 1897.
[52] *Plain Dealer* (Cleveland), March 21, 1897.
[53] Matthew W. Pinkerton, *Murder in All Ages,* p. 479.
[54] *Daily Banner Times* (Greencastle), March 27, 1896.
[55] *Plain Dealer* (Cleveland), March 21, 1897; *Evening Post* (Louisville), February 18, 1897.
[56] *Daily Banner Times* (Greencastle), February 26, 1897.

would be presented at the last minute showing that Walling was not guilty.[57]

Doubt whether Walling was guilty of a capital offense extended even into official circles. Members of the death watch petitioned Governor Bradley to commute Walling's sentence. The governor himself sent word to Sheriff Plummer, who hanged the men, that if Jackson would make a full confession exonerating Walling, even on the scaffold itself, Walling's execution should be postponed until further notice. Jackson refused to make any such confession, and Walling was hanged with him.[58]

After Walling's execution, the Cincinnati *Enquirer* sent a reporter to canvass public opinion in Greencastle. Part of the reporter's story is as follows:

> But there were those who retained the belief that Walling ought not to hang with Jackson. Why he should not they could not support with any sounder argument than their own analysis of evidence and estimate of circumstances that entered into the tragedy. . . . A gentleman of wealth and influence in the community remarked with emphasis: "If Walling is hung it will be legalized murder."
>
> Opposite to this was placed the opinion of another gentleman of like wealth and influence, who said: "Walling is equally guilty with Jackson, and no mercy should be shown one and not the other."
>
> These represented the extremes of belief, and between the two were all the varying shades of opinion, enough to cloud the mind of the brightest lawyer and stupify the most intelligent layman.[59]

Although Walling was convicted of first-degree murder on

[57] *Evening Post* (Louisville), February 18, 1897.
[58] *Plain Dealer* (Cleveland), March 21, 1897; *Enquirer* (Cincinnati), March 21, 1897; *Daily Banner Times* (Greencastle), March 20, 1897.
[59] *Enquirer* (Cincinnati), March 21, 1897.

the same evidence that convicted Jackson, the opinion that Walling was equally guilty with Jackson is here represented as an "extreme" in the spectrum of belief. The two were often lumped together in headlines as "the arch fiends," "heartless fiends," or "murderers Jackson and Walling," but there was a strong tendency to separate them as unequal partners in crime. Scott Jackson was "much brighter than Walling"[60] and "the principal in the crime,"[61] while Walling's face "betrayed the ignorance and the innocence of a weak mentality."[62] To clinch the matter, Jackson had "a head that is said to singularly resemble the head of Holmes, the murderer."[63]

The newspapers and, apparently, the public were convinced of Scott Jackson's guilt, while Walling was a more puzzling and unsatisfying figure. Jackson's motive for the crime was convincing to all, for he was fixed in popular accounts as the father of Pearl's child. Walling had never met Pearl until she came to Cincinnati to procure an abortion. It was difficult to believe that he would help Jackson execute a murder just as a friendly favor, yet this was the only motive the prosecution advanced during Walling's trial.

One possible explanation for Walling's behavior that was not used by the newspapers was that he was simply homicidal. It would not have been an unusual explanation; several famous murderers of the day, including "Holmes, the arch-fiend," and "Durrant, the San Francisco murderer," were characterized as homicidal types who murdered for the pleasure of it.[64] This view

---

[60] *Daily Banner Times* (Greencastle), May 18, 1896.

[61] *Evening Post* (Louisville), February 6, 1896.

[62] *Enquirer* (Cincinnati), March 21, 1897.

[63] *Plain Dealer* (Cleveland), March 21, 1897. See also fn. 64.

[64] William Durrant and Herman W. Mudgett (who murdered under the name of H. H. Holmes) were two celebrated criminals of the 1890's. Holmes, a druggist-cum-real-estate promoter in Chicago, murdered over a dozen lodgers in a gothic castle that he built to accommodate visitors

of Walling was advanced by one professional detective, Matthew W. Pinkerton, of Pinkerton & Company's United States Detective Agency. In a book on murder and murderers, he wrote: "There seems to have been a strong affinity between these two young men, and that it arose from a common lack of all moral principle, a fiendish and most unnatural disposition, cannot well be doubted. . . . The light regard in which they held human life and the brutal manner in which they consummated the terrible crime, argue that they were both victims of the homicidal impulse."[65] This view, however, roused almost no enthusiasm in contemporary and subsequent popular literature. Such an interpretation would make Walling loom as large as Jackson in the story, and this the popular typology could not tolerate. Walling's role as subsidiary murderer, like other stereotyped aspects of the case, derives from something more than the bare facts of the case. Walling was cast as a supporting character rather than as a principal because there was no place for him in the popular conception of what the drama of the murdered girl requires. In the murdered-girl formula the murderer of the girl is her lover. The two forms of popular literature considered in this study—ballads and newspaper stories—were faced with the problem of accommodating to this formula the fact that two men were convicted and executed for the crime. In the ballads, as we shall see, the tendency is usually to forget Walling, sometimes to make of him a subsidiary figure. The approach taken by the papers was to assign to Walling the role of Jackson's tool or

---

to the Chicago World's Fair of 1893. He was finally hanged for his part in an insurance swindle that involved another murder. Durrant, a medical student and Sunday school superintendent in San Francisco, murdered two young ladies in the belfry of his church. The crimes of Holmes and Durrant, as well as that of Jackson and Walling, attracted the epithet "Crime of the Century."

65 Matthew W. Pinkerton, *Murder in All Ages*, p. 480.

puppet. Although two pair of hands may have assisted at Pearl's demise, only one *will* was at work. The story of Pearl Bryan's fate thus becomes an encounter between but two personalities, or two interests—the trusting girl and the lover-murderer.

The facts of the case, as presented in the daily transcripts of court proceedings, suggest that the most likely explanation of Walling's involvement in the crime is as follows: Scott Jackson, and possibly Pearl's cousin Will Wood as well, had been Pearl's lover(s) during the autumn of 1895. When she found herself in an "interesting condition," Pearl appealed for help both to her cousin and to Scott Jackson. Jackson was at that time a dental student in Cincinnati, rooming with Alonzo Walling. Jackson discussed the problem with Walling, who apparently boasted of his prowess in handling such situations, either by locating abortionists or by performing them himself. (This is what Jackson claimed in his court testimony.) Jackson then wrote to Will Wood in Greencastle, telling him to send Pearl to Cincinnati, where they would take care of her. This Wood did. Jackson and Walling attempted an abortion on Pearl, perhaps because their efforts to find a willing doctor failed. But in the course of the operation Pearl either died, or the men thought she had. In desperation, they attempted to prevent identification of the body. They took Pearl's lifeless or semi-lifeless form across the river to Kentucky and beheaded it. They then attempted to dispose of her bloody overclothing, their own bloody clothing, her valise, and the instruments they had used. Their carelessness and delay in doing this provided the principal circumstantial evidence against them.

This explanation is not only consistent with the evidence but also explains the men's unswerving and apparently sincere belief that they did not commit first-degree murder. Walling especially seems to have felt mistreated by the verdict, believing to the end that Jackson might exonerate him. His belief may have been based on a feeling that Pearl was Jackson's problem, not his; and that he had simply tried to help Jackson by attempting the abortion. Although it had failed and Pearl had died, her death was an accident and he was therefore not guilty of murder. Moreover, since it had been done to help Jackson out of a pickle, Jackson owed him protection in the form of some kind of exoneration. The natural tendency for self-justification may have led to some such line of reasoning on Walling's part and would account for his persistent pressure on Jackson to clear him. Apparently Jackson felt there was some justice in this pressure, for on execution day he suddenly announced that he knew Walling was innocent. But, when he realized that he could not say Walling was not present at Pearl's death without admitting that he himself had been present, he retracted his statement. The foregoing interpretation, however, is my own, and is likely to be influenced by late-twentieth-century stereotypes of character and motivation.

Formulaic newspaper reportage covered not only character and motivation, but also the form in which action or incident was presented. The tendency was to portray events in terms of the theater. Newspaper writers consciously presented their reports in terms of "story," "drama," and "scene," as quotations in this chapter show. Even the public in the courtroom at Walling's trial was referred to as an "audience." The story technique is to "leap and linger," as is customary in plays (as well as in "traditional" or "Child" ballads). The reporter dwells at length on significant confrontations between people where action is confined but tension high, and simply summarizes connecting events.

What action is worth lingering over, worth making into a "scene," is predetermined in the Pearl Bryan case by the conventions of the murdered-girl plot. These scenes appeared widely in the newspapers, sometimes again and again. An example is Pearl's sister's celebrated plea for the missing head. This incident was not only reported widely, but it was also almost always selected as one of the features to be included in résumés of the case. Here is an account of the incident from the Cincinnati *Enquirer*:

THE HEADLESS CORPSE

Exhibited to Jackson and Walling—They Accuse Each Other Across the Coffin

One of the most intensely dramatic scenes that has occurred since the discovery of the horrible crime was enacted in Eppley's undertaking establishment on Ninth street, opposite the City Hall, late last evening.

During the afternoon the corpse of the murdered girl was brought from Newport and placed in Eppley's Morgue. The authorities resolved on a plan which they hoped might make the prisoners weaken. It was to have them look upon their murdered victim and have the crime recalled in all its hideousness.

An ENQUIRER reporter accompanied Mayor Caldwell, Colonel Deitsch, and Sheriff Plummer, of Newport, to Eppley's. Shortly after Mrs. J. T. Stanley and young Bryan, the sister and brother of the victim, arrived.

BEFORE THE HEADLESS CORPSE

The remains of the murdered girl were laid out in a pure white casket. The corpse was attired in the silk graduating dress of the poor girl....

In a short time Detectives Crim and McDermott arrived with the prisoners. Crim had Walling in charge and McDermott Jackson. The latter was placed at the head of the coffin and Walling near the foot. Both faced the brother and sister of the murdered girl, who were on the other side of the casket.

... After the men had been given an opportunity to look at the corpse Colonel Deitsch interrogated them:

"Walling, do you recognize the corpse which lies in this casket?" asked Colonel Deitsch in an impressive voice.

"I have every reason to believe it is that of Miss Bryan," responded the prisoner, in a clear voice.

"How do you know that?"

"From what Mr. Jackson has told me."

Turning to Jackson, Colonel Deitsch asked:

"Jackson, do you recognize this corpse?"

"I suppose it is that of Miss Bryan," responded the prisoner in a trembling voice.

"What makes you think so?"

"I see her relatives here."

Turning to Walling, Colonel Deitsch suddenly asked:

"Walling, did you kill this woman?"

"I did not."

"Who did then?"

"I have every reason to believe from what Jackson told me that he did."

Then turning to the other prisoner: "Jackson, did you murder this girl?"

"I did not, sir."

"Can you look upon this corpse and deny that you committed the crime?"

"I can and I do most emphatically," looking nervously at the corpse as he spoke.

"Who did kill her?"

"I have every reason to believe that Walling did."

"You say that you recognize the corpse?"

"I did not say that. I suppose it is, because I see her relatives here."

THE SISTER COULD NOT SPEAK

At this point Colonel Deitsch turned to Mrs. Stanley and asked her if she desired to ask the prisoners any questions. There was a dramatic pause as the lady looked from one prisoner to the other, and then replied in a trembling voice, "I do not, sir."

The same question was put to Fred Bryan, who tried to catch Jackson's eye, but the fellow hung his head and refused to meet his gaze. He, too, declined to question the prisoners.

This ended the scene, and as the officers were preparing to return the men to their cells Sheriff Plummer, of Newport, pulled back the lace around the throat, exposing the ghastly sight. This had no effect on the prisoners, and they were hurried back to their cells.

The scene is one which was probably never before witnessed in this community. It was not thought possible that Jackson at least, could look upon the murdered girl and not weaken. All the ghastly details were brought out, and, to assist in the effect, the brother and sister of the murdered girl consented to be present.

The room was filled with officers and newspaper reporters, and it is safe to say that none of the number were as cool as Walling. This fellow is either one of the most cold-blooded villains in the country, or he is innocent of complicity in the crime. As to this time will tell.

AN AWFUL SCENE

Pearl's Sister Begs the Murderers to Tell Where the Head Is

After the prisoners were taken to Eppley's, where they viewed the remains, and were once more back in their cells, Chief Deitsch decided to send the men to jail. Before doing that he came to the conclusion that he would make one more effort to try and get the prisoners to tell where the head was. Mrs. Stanley, sister of the murdered girl, and her brother were sent for. It was left to them to ask the prisoners. They were sent for and taken into the Lieutenant's room.

There were present Mrs. Stanley, Fred Bryan, Chief Deitsch, Sheriff Plummer, Lieutenant Krumpe and Detectives Crim and McDermott. Jackson was then brought from his cell. He was stood up in front of Mrs. Stanley.

The latter began to cry, and between sobs said:

"Mr. Jackson, I come to you and ask where is my sister's head. For the sake of my poor mother and for my sister and my brother I beg of you to tell me where my sister's head is. It is my last chance and I want to send it home with the body. Won't you please tell me, I beg of you?"

Jackson looked at her, and, without turning a hair, said: "Mrs. Stanley, I don't know."

Not another word was said, and he was taken back to his cell.

Walling was then brought out. Mrs. Stanley was very nervous, as she knew it was the last hope she had. Walling stood up before her, and she asked him to tell her where the head was. She almost begged him on her bended knees to tell, but he coolly replied, "I don't know where it is."

He was locked up, and Mrs. Stanley, and her brother left the station house.

Chief Deitsch came out and said "I've been in many trying situations, but never saw anything to equal that. How they could refuse to tell that poor woman where the head was I cannot understand."[66]

Other newspapers included transcripts of the interchange between Mrs. Stanley and the accused that agreed in substance if not in every detail. A number of reporters were present, and each probably took his own notes of the interview. None of the stories reported that Mrs. Stanley went down on her knees to beg Jackson and Walling for the head, although the *Enquirer* story emphasizes her earnestness in the expression "she almost begged him on her bended knees to tell." A year later, however, the papers unanimously declared in their summaries of the case that "the sister of the dead girl, on her knees, through sobs, pleaded with them to tell where the murdered girl's head was."[67]

66 *Enquirer* (Cincinnati), February 9, 1896.
67 *Plain Dealer* (Cleveland), March 21, 1897.

As anyone familiar with vulgar ballads knows, the standard position in which urgent appeals are made is on the knees. This is also a common gesture in melodrama. Some Pearl Bryan ballads, as we shall see, also focus on this scene and, sharing the same body language as newspaper and melodrama, present Pearl's sister on her knees.

Another scene presented repeatedly in the newspapers was that of Pearl's abandoned body, found accidentally by a farm boy. Whenever there was occasion to summarize the story, this episode was included. One of the shorter versions is the following:

> The sun was just peeking from the horizon, one clear morning, when John Hughlins, a bright-faced country boy, was gayly tripping across field and meadow to his work, near Fort Thomas. He was going to the home of John Lock, a prosperous farmer for whom he worked, when nearing his employer's barn a ghastly sight met his gaze—a few feet away lay the beheaded body of a dead girl!
>
> It lay chest downward, arms outstretched, palms down, fingers half-closed. Above the feet, which were near the gap in the bushes, was a small pool of blood and there was also blood on the leaves of the bushes to the height of nearly three feet. There were stains on top of the leaves, while on the underside were many clots. Nearby was a woman's shoe with a pointed toe, covered by a worn rubber overshoe. Close to the pool of blood on the top of the bank were two or three strands of blonde hair, and near the road two tortoise shell and one metallic hair pin.[68]

The dramatic talents of the news writers were stimulated also by an interview between Mrs. Walling and the Bryan family. Shortly before Walling's execution, Mrs. Walling went to Greencastle to plead with the Bryans to intercede on her son's

[68] *Evening Post* (Louisville), March 20, 1897.

behalf.[69] Although no reporters were present at the interview, this did not stop them from presenting the scene for their readers:

> Standing in the parlor of the pretty home from which Pearl Bryan departed to meet her death, with streaming eyes and quavering voice, Mrs. Walling, the mother of the condemned Alonzo Walling, tonight pleaded with the woman whose torn heart still bleeds for her lost daughter for the life of her son.
>
> It was the last pathetic struggle of mother love, and though more powerful than words can tell it failed absolutely. Though both mothers bewailed their great sorrow in unison, locked in each other's arms, yet sympathy failed to check the resolve of the murdered girl's mother to remain relentless until the slayers of her daughter confess their guilt.[70]

The newspapers never tired of describing courtroom scenes, in which the prisoners and their families confronted the power of the law.

> At 9:35 yesterday morning there was a bustle and craning of necks among the spectators in the Campbell County courtroom.
>
> Scott Jackson, with a jail guard on each side of him, was entering the room to go on trial for his life as the principal in the most atrocious murder of a decade.
>
> Taking a chair, the prisoner shot keen glances over the crowd of spectators in the raised seats, the rows of jurors in the south wing of the courtroom, the lawyers and newspapermen within the rail enclosure and finally fixed a momentary stare upon the slender, youthful-looking judge, as though weighing in his mind

[69] It was assumed by the newspapers that a wish for mercy for the men from the Bryans would affect the governor's decision on their appeals. Evidently, it was felt that the law was exacting justice on behalf of the Bryans, rather than on behalf of society.

[70] *Enquirer* (Cincinnati), March 10, 1897.

the character and disposition of the man who will sentence him or pronounce him free.[71]

Walling unconcernedly fanned himself. He actually smiled as the words that condemned him to death were pronounced. Not so his brothers who sat beside him. Charles leaned heavily on the back of the chair in front of him, and Clinton, pale as death, swayed like a storm-shaken reed. Both cried like children, though not a word was uttered by either. Their sorrow was too deep for words, but, weeping with bitter tears, they sat, silent and in thought, alone.[72]

Nothing in the two trials surpassed in dramatic interest the scene when the jury came in to tender their verdict in Jackson's case. On each side of the prisoner were two armed policemen. All through the room, among the spectators were distributed armed officers in citizen's clothing. Fred Bryan, the murdered girl's brother, took his seat within six feet of the prisoner. The court admonished those present that a large force of officers were distributed through the room. The excitement was intense. Had the verdict been other than murder in the first degree, with the death penalty, there is no knowing what might have happened. At the announcement of the verdict a bare beginning of a demonstration of approval was sternly checked, and in a few minutes the court room was empty and the prisoner in jail.[73]

A sure-fire topic to interest the public, judging by the amount of newspaper space devoted to it, was the last days of Jackson and Walling. Every visit of the grief-stricken families, particularly of the mothers, was described with a wealth of detail. Here is a sample account:

At one o'clock yesterday afternoon Mrs. Walling went to the jail at Alexandria to see her son. She was accompanied by Rev.

[71] Ibid., April 8, 1896.
[72] Ibid., June 19, 1896.
[73] *Evening Post* (Louisville), March 20, 1897.

J. W. Gardner, pastor of the Alexandria Methodist Church, who
had called to see her at Mrs. Orr's residence. Mrs. Wagner, the
kind-hearted jailer's wife, took Mrs. Walling to her own room
while she waited to be admitted to see her son. In the meanwhile
Rev. Gardner had a brief conversation with the prisoners. They
greeted him pleasantly, and the clergyman was much struck by
Jackson's remarkable conversational powers and intellectual appearance.

Mrs. Walling talked about 15 minutes with her son on ordinary subjects. As she was going she stopped and said something
to him in a low tone, pressing her motherly face against the iron
bars. There were tears in her eyes and her lips trembled. Walling could not have replied to her confidence without speaking
so that all in the jail could have heard. He merely said "Good-
bye" and stood gazing at the mother as she parted.[74]

The newspapers occasionally noted the thoughtless remarks
of fellow prisoners or of guards who reminded Jackson and
Walling how few were the days remaining to them. A suffering
mother, however, could do no wrong—witness this sympathetic
presentation of what today would surely be considered monu-
mental tactlessness by Mrs. Jackson:

> Mrs. Jackson told Scott of a strange and awful dream she had
> had Friday night. She said that she had dreamed that he was to
> be executed and the spectacle, with all its horrifying details, was
> presented to her. She saw Sheriff Plummer mount the scaffold
> at the side of her boy, witnessed the placing of the noose about
> his neck, and the black cap drawn over his face. Sheriff Plummer
> then, in Mrs. Jackson's dream, stepped forward and dropped a
> black flag. Mrs. Jackson awoke, being spared in her dream the
> awful finale of the death drop and the dying contortions. The
> recital of the dream had a depressing effect on Jackson, and he

[74] *Enquirer* (Cincinnati), March 6, 1896.

The *Enquirer* Supplement showing personages in the Pearl Bryan trial.

The Evening Post.

"IF NEW AND TRUE, NOT OTHERWISE."

Edition | **Last**

XXXVIII.—NO. 68.   LOUISVILLE, KY., SATURDAY, MARCH 20, 1897.   PRIC

TRANGLED!

and Jackson Executed in Short Order at Newport This Morning.

nor Refused to Interfere and Reprieve Walling at the Last Moment.

onfessed and Said Walling Was Not Guilty of Murder.

THE MURDERERS, THEIR VICTIM AND EXECU

CONFESSED

That Their "Confession" to Gov Bradley Was False.

NO REPRIEVE

Gov Bradley Says It Is Too Late for Him to Interfere.

NOT SATISFIED

The Governor Takes Little Stock in Jackson's Statement.

CONFESSION NO. 2.

Jackson Confesses That He Alone Committed the Murder.

KILLED BY A LOG.

MANSLAUGHTER

Sends John Holloway to the Penitentiary for Four Years

GROWS BITTER

Fight Between Machine and Anti-Machine at Lexington

BLOCKADE TOMORROW.

Liberal Papers Urge England to Keep Out of the Move.

PADUCAH SURROUNDED.

STORY IN DETAIL.

Jackson and Walling Rose Early but Were Not Nervous

The Evening Post reports the execution of Jackson and Walling.

The *Evening Post* sums up the events of the Pearl Bryan murder case.

The *Enquirer* gives the details of the murder.

took his mother's furrowed face in his two hands and kissed her lovingly, and then endeavored to cheer her up by remarking that dreams all go by contraries.[75]

Every detail of the prisoners' last days—how they spent their time, what they said, and what arrangements were being made for the execution—were of interest.

The prison life of the two men is far from being monotonous, though they are compelled to rely on themselves for relief from the monotony. Many hours are whiled away making the muslin ornaments. These decorations have been given to Mrs. Walling, Jailer Wagner and Guards Cottingham, Murray and Sutton. They are now at work on ornaments for Guard Truesdell. In the evening Jackson plays a harmonica and two other prisoners accompany him with mandolin and guitar. The music rendered is really very good. A phonograph is also operated for their amusement during the evening hours. Jackson's taste is to instrumental music, and his favorite selection a banjo duet. Walling inclines to vocal music, and asks every evening for "Au Revoir." A quartet, composed of Guard Sutton, leading: Jackson, tenor, and Walling and Guard Murray, bassos, has been formed, and they can sing very entertainingly "A Mother's Appeal for Her Boy."[76]

[75] Ibid., March 14, 1897.

[76] Ibid. Other choices of songs by the prisoners included "Not Half Has Ever Been Told" and "In the Sweet Bye and Bye." In terms of today's formulae of taste and sensibility, these choices seem a bit bizarre. Since the men steadfastly refused to disclose the whereabouts of Pearl's head, which was in fact never found, one is struck by the title "Not Half Has Ever Been Told." Nor is it my own quirk to note this. An informant wrote me in a letter that Jackson stood on the scaffold and sang this hymn. A reference to it also appears in one composite ballad. Even more striking is the choice "A Mother's Appeal for Her Boy." This song fits well within the criminal-brought-to-justice ballad formula and seems theatrically appropriate on the lips of Scott Jackson. Here follow the words as sung by Charlie Poole and the North Carolina Ramblers in 1929 on Columbia

All these scenes on which the newspapers focussed—the finding of the body, confrontation in the courtroom, the visits in jail, the mother's plea, the last words of the condemned, and the scaffold scene—are familiar ones in American vulgar ballads. The relationship of these scenes in news accounts to these scenes in ballad accounts is discussed in the following chapter.

———

15509-D, under the title "The Mother's Plea for Her Son." (This song is also known as "Don't Send My Boy to Prison.")

[Strolling to?] a courthouse
Not many miles from here
A boy stood in a prison docket
His mother she stood near.

The lad was quite a youngster
Although he'd gone astray
And from his master's cash box
He had stolen some coin away.

The lad addressed His Honor
As the tears flowed down his cheeks
He says "Kind sir, will you please allow
My mother here to speak?"

The Honor then consented
While the boy hung down his head
And turning to the jury then
These words his mother said:

"Remember I'm a widow
And the prisoner is my son
And gentlemen remember
This is the first crime he has done.

Don't send my boy to prison
For that would drive me mad
Remember I'm a widow
And I'm pleading for my lad."

The widow's eye was flashing fire
And her cheek turned deathly pale
"The reason why I'm here today
To save my boy from jail.

Although I know he's guilty
And know his crime is bad
But remember I'm his mother
And I'm pleading for my lad.

Remember I'm a widow
And the prisoner is my son
And gentlemen remember
It is the first crime he has done.

Don't send my boy to prison
For that would drive me mad
Remember I'm a widow
I'm pleading for my lad."

Note the similarities between this text and that of Pearl Bryan V, given on pages 63–67—especially Text II, sixth verse. Compare also the following headline from the Cincinnati *Enquirer* for March 10, 1897:

REFUSED
A Mother's Appeal
Mrs. Walling Pleads for Her Erring Boy's Life

3. THE BALLADS

Poor Pearl! poor girl
She thought she was going right
She had no dream of murder
On that dark stormy night.

We have seen so far how newspaper accounts of the Pearl Bryan case were influenced by formulae. These formulae included set sequences of words, such as "aged parents" and "poor Pearl"; set characters, such as the grief-ridden parent and the innocent, trusting girl; set scenes, such as the pleading on bended knee and a weeping mother's visit to her son in jail; and even an entire plot formula: artful man seduces innocent girl; when he learns she is pregnant he lures her to a secluded spot; she offers little resistance to being murdered; he abandons her body.

This chapter will show the same formulae at work in ballad versions of the story. Newspaper accounts and ballad accounts share formulae in every category listed above: set sequences of words, set characters, set scenes, and set plot.

There was a rival plot formula that for a time competed for control of the Pearl Bryan story, but without significant success. This formula might be called the "criminal-brought-to-justice" formula. It appears often in American balladry, commonly in the forms called "last goodnight" or "confession" ballads. The criminal-brought-to-justice formula contains the following elements: youth, upbringing, or past deeds of the criminal; the crucial crime and what brings the criminal to it; capture, trial, and imprisonment; execution, usually by hanging.[1] Particularly attracted to this type of ballad are such scene formulae as jail scenes, weeping-relative scenes, courtroom scenes, and scaffold scenes.

Only the second half of the criminal-brought-to-justice formula appears in the Pearl Bryan ballads: the capture-trial-imprisonment and the hanging. What appears before that follows the murdered-girl formula. By and large, the criminal aspects of the ballads tend to grow weaker, and the murdered-girl aspects stronger.

The relationship between newspaper and ballad accounts of the story does not consist simply of independent reliance on the same formulae. There can be little doubt that composers of Pearl Bryan ballads got their information about the case from news stories. This conclusion is based on several arguments.

The newspapers were a readily available source for information, and a popular one. The Pearl Bryan case was widely discussed in Indiana, Ohio, and Kentucky, and the newspapers were eagerly awaited each day. Six months after the trial of Walling, the Greencastle *Daily Banner Times* carried the following paragraph:

[1] Ballads about criminals need not be of the criminal-brought-to-justice type. There is, for example, an "outlaw" type, which follows a different formula. A series of exploits of the outlaw are related. A final episode describes his death, often by betrayal. Examples are "Jesse James," "Sam Bass," "Cole Younger," "The Wild Colonial Boy," and "Brennan on the Moor." The outlaw is usually not brought to trial but dies with his boots on, shooting it out with the law if he is not shot in the back. The criminal of the criminal-brought-to-justice formula usually commits one crime, and his life is ground out slowly by legal machinery.

The importance which politics plays in the life of Kentucky, is well illustrated by the fact that all proceedings in the Jackson and Walling murder case was [sic] postponed until after the election. Four months ago the entire state was discussing the trials of the two murderers of Pearl Bryan, and the mystery surrounding the Fort Thomas crime was the topic of conversation on the street corners of every town and hamlet of Kentucky into which the daily papers of Cincinnati and Louisville carried their daily story. Even the country papers of the state, including the remoter counties, printed many columns regarding the two prisoners and their trials at Newport.[2]

Not only were the papers a readily available source, but they also were perhaps the only readily available source. Not many people from the three deeply interested states could come to court each day during the trials of Jackson and Walling. The courtrooms were often crowded, especially on days when some "sensation" was expected; but, just as often, reporters at the trials remarked how few spectators were present. The Louisville *Evening Post* had this explanation: "The trial of Jackson attracted as much attention as any ever held in the United States. There were newspaper men from all parts of the country. Nearly everybody living near Newport was present, or attempted to be present, at sometime during the trial. Their morbid desire was not the result so much to hear the evidence as to see the prisoner, and after getting a good look at him left the courtroom."[3]

Scanty attendance at Walling's trial was particularly marked.[4] Yet the two men apparently were excellent copy and sold a lot of newspapers.[5] For thirteen months scarcely a day

[2] *Daily Banner Times* (Greencastle), November 6, 1896.

[3] *Evening Post* (Louisville), March 20, 1897.

[4] Ibid.

[5] *Daily Banner Times* (Greencastle), March 16, 22, 1897.

passed without some news story appearing about the men, including items on what they had to eat, what activities they pursued, and what they said to visitors. While the public was deeply interested in Jackson and Walling, it was not interested in wading through the mass of evidence. From the beginning Jackson was established as guilty and Walling as an accessory at least, and public interest centered primarily on human interest details.

Aside from news stories and personal attendance at the trials, a source from which potential balladeers might have drawn information is rumor or personal reports. It is apparent that a great deal of discussion and rumor did animate the public during these famous trials. But if such reports were sources for ballad information, they either came from newspaper accounts originally or were themselves sources for newspaper accounts. All the information in the ballads that is specific to the Pearl Bryan case rather than to the murdered-girl formula is identical to information appearing in newspapers. At times the ballads display startlingly detailed correspondences with newspaper stories. One ballad describes the use of bloodhounds in an attempt to find Pearl's head:

> Next morning the people were excited
> For miles around and said
> Here lies a woman's body
> But we can not find her head
>
> .   .   .   .
>
> Bloodhounds were placed upon the trail
> No answer so they said
> Pearl Bryan's body has gone to rest
> But we can not find her head
>
> .   .   .   .
>
> Policemen and detectives
> The can they drained and said

> God bless her, she's gone to rest
> But we can not find her head[6]

These three verses summarize exactly what was reported in the newspapers in the days following discovery of the body. The "next morning" after the murder, the body was discovered. Cincinnati people showed great interest in the discovery, many coming to the spot where the body was found, in order to poke around for clues and to carry away blood-stained privet leaves as souvenirs. The next day a famous trio of bloodhounds, Stonewall, Wheeler, and Jack, were brought from Indiana to trace the missing head. The trail led to Covington Reservoir Number Two and stopped. While hundreds of Cincinnatians stood in a cold drizzle to watch, police drained the reservoir, under the direction of two Cincinnati detectives. No head was found.

During these first few days after the discovery of the body, the newspapers were full of speculation about the hiding place of the head. After a time, the police were so desperate to find the head that they followed the directions of spiritualists and prophetic dreams, but these proved no more successful than the usual avenues of police investigation. The ballad's repeated, refrain-like line, "But we can not find her head," perfectly reflects the consternation and preoccupation of Cincinnati police and citizens at that time.

Perhaps the most startling piece of accurate and detailed reportage in the ballads appears in the following lines:

Jackson wrote a letter to Willie Wood one day
Told him to write another to Pearl's home and say

[6] "The Murder of Pearl Bryan," in W. C. Herd, *Comic and Sentimental Songs*, a pocket songster bought about 1910 in Murray, Kentucky. On file in the Western Kentucky Folklore Archive at the University of California, Los Angeles.

"I'm not in Indianapolis," and sign her name you may
You stick to your old chum, Bill, and I will help you some day.[7]

The letter to which the song refers is one written by Jackson
to Will Wood, Pearl's cousin, and intercepted at the time of
Wood's arrest. (Wood was at first suspected of complicity in
the crime.) The letter was widely printed in newspapers and
also appeared in evidence at Jackson's trial. The relevant por-
tions of that letter are as follows:

> Hello Bill,
>
> Write a letter home signed by Bert's name, telling the folks
> that he is somewhere and going to Chicago or some other place
> —has a position, etc.—and that they will advise later about it.
> . . . Tell the folks that he has not been at I., . . . Stick by your
> old chum, Bill, and I will help you out the same way or some
> other way some time.[8]

"Bert," as Scott Jackson and Will Wood acknowledged, referred
to Pearl Bryan and was a precautionary name used by them in
their letters. "I." referred to Indianapolis.

From these examples it is clear that at least some of the Pearl
Bryan ballads drew directly on news stories for their information. The appearance of the same formulae in ballads and news
stories may not be independent. Some topical ballads appear to
be simply rhymed versions of formulae already presented in
newspapers.

To show the workings of these formulae in the ballads requires chronological as well as synchronic examination of the
texts. The increasing power of the murdered-girl formula is
argued from the history of the texts, given below. Two assump-

[7] From the singing of Mrs. Effie Carmack; recorded by Austin Fife at
Atascadero, California. On file in the Western Kentucky Folklore Archive
at the University of California, Los Angeles.

[8] E.g., *Star-Press* (Greencastle), February 15, 1896.

tions have been made about the texts, as an occasional aid in dating them:

1. The closer in time a topical ballad is to its subject, the more likely it is to contain correct details about the event. Conversely, the more distant in time a topical ballad is from its subject, the more prone it is to lose or falsify detail. This is not to say that astonishingly correct details do not survive, but only that it is more remarkable in a ballad longer in tradition.

2. As time passes, the language of a ballad that is sung is more likely to become simple and singable than complex and literary; complex sentences will tend to become simple ones, and literary expressions not found in common speech will tend to become confused and garbled, if not replaced or omitted.

In *Native American Balladry*,[9] Laws distinguishes four different ballads about Pearl Bryan. He knows of at least one more, for he quotes it in one of his analytical chapters.[10] But there is no evidence that this one went into oral tradition. Of the four, one is considered of doubtful currency in oral tradition, and another is an adaptation of the popular murdered-girl ballad "The Jealous Lover." It is the contention of this study that there are, or were, at least six Pearl Bryan ballads in oral tradition and that through selective borrowing and fusing they evolved into two main families or strains, those labelled by Laws Pearl Bryan I and Pearl Bryan II.

Taking them in order, I will consider the evidence for dividing the Pearl Bryan texts into six types, accepting in the main Laws' assignment of numbers to Pearl Bryans I through IV, and adding types V and VI. Once the case for dividing the texts into six types is made, the chapter outlines the histories of the six types.

Before so doing, a note is in order about my grounds for di-

[9] G. Malcolm Laws, Jr., *Native American Balladry*, pp. 191–193, 270.
[10] Ibid., p. 33.

viding the ballads into a set of types somewhat different from those established by Laws. First of all, I had many more texts to work from than Laws did, including over two dozen unpublished texts from the Library of Congress, a similar number from the Western Kentucky Folklore Archive, and nine I collected myself. On the basis of this larger number of texts I believe it is reasonable to add numbers V and VI to the list and to claim that some of the verses Laws ascribes to I are actually a part of V. The one text in his list that includes these verses is an uncommon instance of borrowing—a fusion of half of I with half of V.[11]

Laws distinguishes three of his four Pearl Bryan ballads on the basis of plot elements. The difficulty with such a scheme, as Laws himself realizes, is that it is possible to have two ballads with identical plots that are not at all the same. Language, tone, style, point of view, clichés—all could be different. To alleviate this difficulty, Laws gives a characteristic verse or two from each ballad to help identify it.

It seems that the only unambiguous way to identify a ballad is by enumeration—by saying, in effect, "Ballad A consists of the following verses, and any change is a variation of the ballad." The parallel difficulty with this method is that what is gained in clarity is lost in accuracy. For there is no one "correct" text for a ballad, with all others being corruptions.

What we have at hand is a number of texts, some of which are clearly related, and sometimes nearly identical, to each other. They seem to fall naturally into groups. At the same time, we see that verses or groups of verses that normally appear in one context will occasionally turn up in a different context. The natural assumption is that these verses were "borrowed" by the other ballad and that they do not normally "belong" to it. Certainly we must admit that, unless all the Pearl Bryan verses

[11] Brewster, "A" text, *Ballads and Songs from Indiana*, p. 283.

are fragments of one enormous and kaleidoscopic original, the fact that the same verse may turn up in two entirely different compositions shows that borrowing does indeed take place.

If a text turns up composed of five verses normally found only in Pearl Bryan I, followed by five verses normally found only in Pearl Bryan V, I assume that the composer of the ballad stitched together his new ballad from elements of the two others. It is possible, but unreasonable, to assume that this novelty is the original ballad, that it split into two parts, that each of these parts accrued additional verses, and that the two new ballads then became more widespread than the parent ballad. In the absence of other evidence, I have assumed the first process with each such cross-bred text.

Nevertheless, such texts sometimes have a hybrid vigor that enables them to outlive their ancestors. At this point, the numbering system is strained. If Pearl Bryans I and V are distinct for many years and then begin to fuse, how are we to indicate this in the numbering system? If Pearl Bryan I consists from the beginning of several verses borrowed from Pearl Bryan VI as well as others from another source, and if Pearl Bryan I survives while Pearl Bryan VI withers away, how are we to indicate this in the numbering system? Fortunately, in the case of the Pearl Bryan ballads the types have remained distinct enough so that the numbers do form a rough guide to the contents of the texts. Hybrids can be indicated by such locutions as "I x V."

Another difficulty in characterizing the types is that, in the case of Pearl Bryan II, no one text contains all the verses appearing frequently in the texts. In the case of this ballad I have set up a check list consisting of all the verses appearing in at least two independent collected texts. The double appearance of a verse is my minimum standard for classifying a verse as traditional in a particular ballad.

One claim for the following reorganization of the ballad types is that it is useful. In this scheme of classification there are fewer anomalous cases and fewer instances of clearly differing texts jammed into the same pigeonhole because of certain shared verses. Further, this classification represents real historical types that interacted to produce the two strains most widespread today. With this system of numbered types I can refer conveniently to those ballads whose development in terms of the murdered-girl pattern I wish to show.

Pearl Bryan I

Of the 135 texts of traditional ballads about Pearl Bryan known to me, 23 are clearly of the type labelled by Laws as Pearl Bryan I. Another 7 texts contain some verses normally found in Pearl Bryan I and some verses normally found in one of the other types. The 23 texts of type I can be further divided into two groups: those which derive from recordings made by the enormously popular Vernon Dalhart and released in 1927, and those which have another common source. There are 11 texts in the first group and 11 in the second, while one other text is basically in the first group but shows two points of cross-influence from the second. The two groups are distinguished by minor differences, but these differences are consistent throughout. These groups are designated "Dalhart" and "non-Dalhart." A model text for each group is given below.

Dalhart

Now ladies, if you listen
A story I'll relate
That happened near Fort Thomas
In old Kentucky State

'Twas late in January
This awful deed was done

By Jackson and by Walling
How cold their blood did run

How bold these cruel villains
To do this awful deed
To hide away Pearl Bryan
When she to them did plead

The driver tells the story
Of how Pearl Bryan did moan
From Cincinnati to the place
Where the cruel deed was done

But little did Pearl's parents think
When she left her happy home
That their own darling daughter
Would ne'er return again

We know her dear old parents
Their fortune they would give
If Pearl could just return home
A happy life to live

The driver was the only one
Could tell her awful fate
Of poor Pearl far away from home
In the old Kentucky State

A farmer passing by next day
Her lifeless form he found
A-lying on the cold sod
Where her blood had stained the ground

Pearl Bryan left her parents
On a dark and gloomy day
She went to meet the villain
In a spot not far away

She thought it was the lover's hand
That she could trust each day
Alas! it was a lover's hand
That took her life away

Young ladies now take warning
Young men are so unjust
It may be your best lover
But you know not whom to trust

Pearl died away from home and friends
Out in that lonely spot
Take heed, take heed, believe this girls
Don't let this be your lot.[12]

Non-Dalhart

Young ladies if you listen
Now a story relate
It happened near Fort Thomas
In the old Kentucky State

It was January the thirty-first
This awful deed done
By Jack Walling and Pearl Bryon
How cold their blood did run

Cho: How bolden were those wicked men
To do this lone-some deed
To hide away Pearl Bryon's head
When she to them did plead

Little did Pearl Bryon think
On a dark and gloomy day
The grip she carried in her hand
Would hide her head away

She thought it was a lover's hand
She could trust both night and day
Alas! it was her lover's hand
That took her life away

[12] As sung by Vernon Dalhart under the pseudonym of Jep Fuller on Vocalion 5015, recorded October 5, 1926, and released in 1927.

The driver in the seat is all,
Who can tell the dread-ful fate
Of poor Pear Bryon far from home,
In the old Kentucky State

How sad it must have been for him
To hear Pearl's lonely voice
At midnight at that lonely place
Where those two men rejoiced

Little did Pearl's parents think,
When she left her happy home
Their darling girl in her youth
Would nevermore return

Her aged parents we all know
Their fortune they would give
If Pearl again returned to them,
Her natural life to live

The driver Jackson tells the story,
How poor Pearl Bryon did moan
From Cincinnati to the place
Where the dreadful deed was done

Next day a farmer passing by
Spied a lifeless form
A lying on the cold damp ground
And the blood stained all around

Young ladies all take warning,
Young men are so unjust
He may be your best lover,
And know not whom to trust

Pearl died away from home and friends,
Upon a lonely spot
My God! My God! believe this girls,
Don't let this be your lot.[13]

[13] Text sent to me by Mrs. Clara Nussbaumer, West Unity, Ohio, in July 1966. Her title for the song is "Pearl Bryon."

The non-Dalhart group of texts always specifies the date of the crime—"January the thirty-first"—while the Dalhart group gives the time as "late in January."

The Dalhart group, in both its second and third verses, refers to the crime as an "awful deed," while the non-Dalhart group usually refers to it as a "dreadful deed" and sometimes as an "awful deed." Moreover, the second reference to the crime may be "lawless deed," "lowest deed," "lowly deed," or "lonesome deed." "Terrible deed" makes one appearance. The non-Dalhart group may have two "dreadfuls," or a "dreadful" and an "awful," or a "dreadful/awful" and a "lawless-lowest-lowly-lonesome," but never two "awfuls."

The Dalhart group invariably refers to Pearl's fate as her "awful fate." Pearl's fate appears only twice in the non-Dalhart group, but as "dreadful fate" and "sad fate." In addition, the Dalhart group refers to the murderers as "cruel villains," an expression never found in the non-Dalhart group. If an epithet is used, it is "wretched men" or "wicked men."

The non-Dalhart group includes a verse indicating that Pearl's suitcase was destined to carry her head; the Dalhart group does not mention Pearl's headlessness at all, while the non-Dalhart group always includes it. The non-Dalhart group includes a verse about the cabman hearing Pearl's voice pleading with the murderers; the Dalhart group has no such verse.

Those of the non-Dalhart versions which include the verse given last in the model text use the expression "my God" or "my God, my God." The one exception simply says, "Believe this girls." The Dalhart group always substitutes "take heed, take heed" for "my God, my God."

All in all, the Dalhart group is much more homogeneous than the non-Dalhart group; the verses are almost always in order and complete. This suggests that learning from an unvarying source, such as a phonograph record, produces texts that are more fixed than those learned from the usual oral process.[14]

I am certain that the non-Dalhart version is the earlier one and that Dalhart's writer, Carson Robison, made slight changes in the words of an existing broadside for Dalhart's use. Evidence for this is seen in the files of the Vocalion Record Company, for whom Dalhart made his first recording of the ballad "Pearl Bryan." The company's ledger sheets, usually filled out shortly after recordings were made, called for composer and copyright data. In the case of Dalhart's "Pearl Bryan," the "composer" column contained the notation "words—? Tune— 'Little Mary Phagan'." Opposite the tune entry was noted, in the "copyright" column, "Carson & Carson, Polk G. Brockman, 1925." At this period in his career, most of Dalhart's topical ballads were written by Carson J. Robison.[15] Thus, the Vocalion ledger sheets suggest that on October 5, 1926, when Dalhart, accompanied by Robison, recorded "Pearl Bryan," Robison did not know whether a copyright was held on the words. He certainly would have copyrighted them himself if he had written them. The fact that Robison used the tune to an already existing murdered-girl ballad may mean that he had in hand a printed broadside which he wanted Dalhart to record, but for which he had no tune. To my knowledge, "Little Mary Phagan"

[14] The one exception that does not meet all these criteria is in every respect a Dalhart version except that it has "January the 31st" instead of "late in January" in the first line and has two "dreadful deeds" instead of two "awful deeds." This text was printed in the *Renfro Valley Bugle*, July 1965, with no information as to its source. The heading under which it was printed read "From the Library."

[15] Some of Robison's ballads have since become traditional (e.g., "Naomi Wise" and "Wreck of the No. 9"). On the other hand, Robison was not above copyrighting older traditional material (e.g., "Barbara Allen").

was not at that time a traditional tune for Pearl Bryan I; the non-Dalhart texts for which I have tunes do not use it.

Three weeks after the Vocalion recording date, when Dalhart and Robison recorded this ballad for Columbia, the composer credits were given to "Robison-Thompson." Perhaps Robison had by this time assured himself that the words were in the public domain; or, again, the unidentified "Thompson" may have been the author of the broadside Robison modified for Dalhart.

Although Pearl Bryan I is a relatively popular ballad on the subject, second only to Pearl Bryan II in number of collected texts, it does not appear in the forms given here until 1927, at which time it appears in both forms. All the Pearl Bryan ballads except I and the rare IV have been either collected before 1927 or dated by one or more informants before 1927. Pearl Bryan I is neither collected nor dated by informants before 1927. Some of the individual verses found in Pearl Bryan I, however, did circulate before 1927. Four times they appear here and there in texts collected earlier, where they are found attached to what I have labelled Pearl Bryans V and VI.

An explanation is wanted for the sudden appearance in 1927 of two remarkably stable and popular variants of a ballad, while before that time we find only occasional floating verses of it. I conclude that at some time between 1920 and 1926 a broadside was circulated containing a new song (my Pearl Bryan I), some of whose verses came from an older ballad and some of which were perhaps newly composed. I think that the older ballad on which Pearl Bryan I drew was Pearl Bryan VI and that its choice of verses from that ballad shows the influence of the murdered-girl pattern. Pearl Bryan VI contains elements of both the murdered-girl and the criminal-brought-to-justice formulae, while Pearl Bryan I is entirely of the murdered-girl type. This will be developed further in the discussion of Pearl Bryan VI below.

PEARL BRYAN II

This group has by far the greatest number of Pearl Bryan ballads, comprising 65 of the 135 texts known to me. There have been collected, in addition, 9 fragments of this ballad and 2 texts in which verses from this ballad have been attached to other Pearl Bryan ballads.

Pearl Bryan II usually consists of the standard "Jealous Lover" stanzas,[16] with the names of Pearl Bryan and Scott Jackson inserted at appropriate points. In three collected versions, however, a distinctly different verse is added, an inappropriate "friendship verse" normally found in autograph albums.[17] The three texts containing this verse were collected in 1928, 1956, and 1964. It is possible that the source for this intrusion is a 1927 recording made by Richard Burnett and Leonard Rutherford, both folk/hillbilly performers from Kentucky.[18] It is also possible that the intrusion comes from Burnett's own source, for in a 1962 interview he said that a friend taught him the song from a book.[19] This verse is found frequently in Pearl Bryan V, appearing first in a text dated 1932.

No one text of Pearl Bryan II contains all the verses that appear frequently in the various collected texts. Therefore, I have

[16] Laws F 1; see Laws, p. 191.

[17] Two versions of the verse are given in an article on Ozark friendship verses, written by Vance Randolph and Mary Kennedy McCord, *Journal of American Folklore* 61 (1948): 187.

[18] Burnett and Rutherford, "Pearl Bryan," Columbia 15113-D.

[19] Taped interview with Richard Burnett at Monticello, Ky., August 17, 1962, by Gene Earle and Archie Green. A copy of the tape is at the John Edwards Memorial Foundation at the University of California, Los Angeles.

set up a check list of all verses appearing at least twice in collected texts; it follows now, in lieu of a sample collected text.

Deep, deep in yonders valley
Where the flowers fade and bloom
There lies poor Pearl Bryan
In a cold and silent tomb

She died not broken hearted
Nor lingering ill befell
But in an instant parted
From one she loved so well

One night the moon shone brightly
The stars were shining too
When to her cottage window
Her jealous lover drew

Come Pearl, let's take a ramble
O'er the meadows wide and gay
Where no one will disturb us
We'll name our wedding day

Deep, deep into the valley
He led his love so dear
Says she, "It's for you only
That I am rambling here

"The way seems dark and dreary
And I'm afraid to stay
Of rambling I've grown weary
And would retrace my way"

"Retrace your way? No, never!
These woods no more you'll roam
So bid farewell forever
To parents, friends and home

"You have not the wings of an eagle
Nor from me can you fly
No human hand can aid you
Pearl Bryan you must die"

"What have I done, Scott Jackson
That you should take my life?
You know I've always loved you
And would have been your wife"

There's room for my name in your album
There's room for my love in your heart
There's room for us both in heaven
Where true friends never part

Down on her knees before him
She pleaded for her life
But into her snow white bosom
He plunged a fatal knife

"Farewell my loving parents
My happy peaceful home
Farewell my dear old schoolmates
With you no more I'll roam

"Farewell my dear, dear sister
My face you'll see no more
Long, long you'll wait my coming
At the little cottage door

"But Jackson I'll forgive you
With my last and dying breath"
Her pulse had ceased their beating
Her eyes were closed in death

The birds sang in the morning
But doleful were their songs
A stranger found Pearl Bryan
Cold headless on the ground.

Pearl Bryan III

Pearl Bryan III has been collected six times, once as a fragment. There is little variation among the texts. A sample text is given below.

In Green Castle lived a lady
Who was known this wide world o'er
Who was courted by Scott Jackson
Whom she fondly did adore

Yes, she loved him, truly loved him,
And they both being young and gay
And she trusted in him fondly
And by him was led astray

When she told him her sad story,
And him knowing it was true,
Held his head for just one moment,
For he knew not what to do

Then he called on his friend Walling
For to seek advice and aid
And they held a consultation
And this dying plot was made

In a cab one rainy evening,
At the closing of the day,
Up drove Walling and Scott Jackson
And with Pearl they drove away

This young girl with all her beauty
Left the city with these men
Little did she think that moment
What would be her woeful end

Yes they took her from this city
Far away from friends and home,
And they left her body lying
Headless, blood stain, all alone

Yes they killed her, surely killed her,
It's been known this wide world o'er
And the murder of Pearl Bryan
Has been told in words before.[20]

20 "Pearl Bryan," from Miss Audrey Cline, Rinard Mills, Ohio; in

Pearl Bryan IV

This ballad so seldom appears that it is doubtful whether it ever had much currency in oral tradition. It has been collected twice complete and once as a two-line fragment in a conglomerate text.[21] A model text appears below.

In Greencastle, Indiana, a fair young maiden dwelled
  Beneath a mother's loving care, a father's lavish wealth,
A mother's pride, a father's joy, by many friends esteemed,
  From out of her young handsome face the pure innocence
    gleamed.

One day she met a lover gay, she thought him kind and true,
  "My love," she said, "I'd rather die than live away
    from you."
She loved him with a love that mothers give her only babe,
  She saw him midst her sweetest dream, and thought of
    him awake.

The maiden soon of him did plead a great wrong for to right
  "I thought now you will not, dearest, leave me in my
    present plight";
He only smiled and answered her, "Young girl you loved
    too true,
  I leave you now, farewell, we part, adieu, part,
    love, adieu."

Rather than face her many friends, she followed in his path;
  He led her to a lonely spot, and awful was his wrath;

Robert W. Gordon, unpublished mss. at the Library of Congress, Washington, D.C.

[21] An unusual ballad about Pearl Bryan, made up of verses from IV, V, and VI, plus elements from the popular song "The Band Played On," was recorded by Ed Kahn in 1958 at Parksville, Ky., from the playing of Forrest Lewis. It is curious that this conglomeration, which Lewis said he learned from his father, contains verses from the less popular Pearl Bryans and omits the widespread I and II.

But little did he think that far above in the blue sky
   A witness there who sees a crime with an all-seeing eye.

All night a headless body lay aside a lonely street
   Suspicion points to three young men as having done the deed;
The evidence does plainly implicate all three of them,
   For more atrocious crime no man did ever hang.

This crime does teach a lesson true, young girls I pray
      take heed
   Your mother is the truest friend you'll find in times
      of need;
The story will be oftentimes told by friends from time to time,
   Of Scott Jackson along a Walling, Will Wood, and poor
      Pearl Bryan.[22]

It is understandable that this ballad was not popular in tradition, for it is virtually unsingable. One of the two texts shows some signs of oral processing, as some of the more unwieldy locutions are simplified.

PEARL BRYAN V

Of the sixteen texts I have classified as Pearl Bryan V, four texts and three fragments have been collected that share no verses with other Pearl Bryan ballad types. Nine texts and two fragments share verses with Pearl Bryans I, II, and VI. Of these nine, five share a particular pair of verses with Pearl Bryan II; two share a verse found in both Pearl Bryan VI and non-Dalhart I; and two share all three of these verses. The two verses shared with Pearl Bryan II are the following:

> What have I done, Scott Jackson
> That you should take my life?
> You know I always loved you
> And would have been your wife

---

[22] "A Fatal Acquaintance," from Mrs. Rozetta Lozier, Perrysville, Ohio, in Mary O. Eddy, *Ballads and Songs from Ohio*, p. 241.

Is there room for my name in your album?
Is there room for my love in your heart?
There's room for us both in heaven
Where true lovers never part

The verse shared with Pearl Bryan VI and non-Dalhart I is the following:

Little did Pearl Bryan think
When she left her home that day
That the grip she carried in her hand
Would carry her head away

The above verse, which appears three times in Pearl Bryan V, might have been borrowed from either Pearl Bryan I or Pearl Bryan VI. It is my contention that Pearl Bryan VI is prior to I, and that I was composed partially of borrowings from VI. Thus the verse that V shares with I and VI can be considered a borrowing, ultimately, from VI. I think it probable that V is older than I; hence, V probably got this verse directly from VI rather than indirectly from I. It is possible, however, that this particular verse was not part of V in its original form, but was a later borrowing from I; for all three texts of Pearl Bryan V containing this verse appear after 1929, while Pearl Bryan I in the form we have it appears suddenly in 1926–1927. The popularity of Pearl Bryan I, and its frequent recording on hillbilly records, must be considered.

The pair of verses that Pearl Bryan V shares with Pearl Bryan II is puzzling. The first member of the pair, the "what-have-I-done" verse, is almost invariably found in both Pearl Bryan II and "The Jealous Lover" from which it derives. The second member of the pair, the "album" verse, is found in only three out of seventy-seven texts and fragments of Pearl Bryan II, while it is found in seven out of sixteen texts and fragments of Pearl Bryan V. Wherever the "album" verse appears in Pearl

Bryan V, it is in association with the "what-have-I-done" verse.

It would appear, then, that the "album" verse is better established in Pearl Bryan V than in Pearl Bryan II, even though it appears in association with a verse (the "what-have-I-done" verse) that is clearly from Pearl Bryan II. Since the "album" verse does not appear in "The Jealous Lover" or in any of the other Pearl Bryan ballads, we can assume that it originated in either II or V and was borrowed by the other. I do not think that this verse was a part of the earliest forms of either ballad, for it does not make an appearance in Pearl Bryan II until 1926–1927, in a commercial recording, and not in Pearl Bryan V until 1929. The earliest date given to Pearl Bryan II is 1903–1905, and the earliest date given to Pearl Bryan V is about 1910.

Internal evidence suggests that Pearl Bryan V was composed by someone familiar with newspaper stories of the case. The earliest date that can be given a text is 1910. This text comes from a pocket songster a Kentucky informant said he bought around 1910. It contains most of the verses found in other texts of Pearl Bryan V and also has an additional verse showing knowledge of contemporary events:

> Policemen and detectives
> The can they drained and said
> God bless her, she's gone to rest
> But we cannot find her head

This verse contains the only mention in any of the Pearl Bryan ballads of the draining of the Covington reservoir in the hope of finding Pearl's head.

Early texts of Pearl Bryan V describe in detail the excitement in Cincinnati when the body was found, the attempts to identify it, the use of bloodhounds to find the head, and the plea Pearl's sister made to Jackson to reveal where he had put the head. This ballad also relates, though in distorted form, the

last-minute attempts of Walling's mother to save him.[23] Later
texts of Pearl Bryan V begin to omit the bloodhounds, the attempts to identify the body, and the attempts to find the head.
The pleas of Mrs. Walling and Pearl's sister are more persistent,
but Mrs. Walling's plea is not always found. The most vigorous
feature of this ballad is the plea of Pearl's sister; it not only per-
sists in Pearl Bryan V but is the most frequently borrowed
element of the ballad. The fourth verse of the first text of Pearl
Bryan V given below derives from the chorus of a popular song,
"The Baggage Coach Ahead." This song was composed by a
one-time Cincinnati janitor and train porter, Gussie L. Davis,
and was published in 1896. One other text also shows intrusion
from a popular song of the same period. In 1958 Forrest L.
Lewis of Parksville, Kentucky, played for Ed Kahn a Pearl
Bryan ballad he had learned from his father. His text uses the
chorus from "The Band Played On," a popular song composed
by J. F. Palmer and C. B. Ward, published in 1895. The double
intrusion into Pearl Bryan V of snatches from popular songs of
1895–1896 suggests that Pearl Bryan V might have been composed while these songs were in vogue, shortly before the turn
of the century.

Below are two texts for Pearl Bryan V, which between them
cover all the verses common to the type.

Text I

> Twas late one winter's evening
> The sorrowful tale was told
> Scott Jackson says to Lonz Wallon
> Let's go out for a stroll.

[23] In March 1897, Mrs. Walling traveled to Greencastle to plead with
the Bryans to intercede on Walling's behalf. She begged the same favor
of Governor W. O. Bradley. Both refused. Her unavailing attempts were
portrayed sympathetically and at length by the newspapers, as described
in Chapter 2.

Wallon answered softly
While strolling by his side
Let's take the lady fair
Pearl Bryant for a ride.

A cab then was ordered
For them to take a stroll
And if you'll only listen
The half has not been told.

The cab then arriving
Pearl Bryant sat in tears
Thinking of the happiness
She had had in the last few years.

Oh what have I done Scott Jackson
For you to take my life
You know that I always loved you
And would have been your wife.

There's room for your name in my album
There's room for your love in my breast
There's room for us both in heaven
Where true lovers will evermore rest.

Early early next morning
The people gathered round
Says here lies a woman's body
But her head cannot be found.

The bloodhounds then were ordered
To tell the trail they said
Here lies a woman's body
But we can't find her head.

In came Pearl Bryant's sister
To-falling on her knees
A-pleading with Scott Jackson
Her sister's head, oh please.

Jackson sets there stubborn
Not a word then he said
When I meet my sister in heaven
There'll be no missing head.

In came Lonz Wallon's mother
A-pleading for her son
A-pleading to the jurors
For the first crime he'd ever done.

The jurors made no answer
But to their feet they sprung
Says for the crime the boys committed
The boys must be hung.

'Twas on the thirtieth day of January
The sorrowful crime was done
Scott Jackson and Lonz Wallon
Pearl Bryant's life they won.

So now young ladies take warning
Before it is too late
Of the crime that the boys committed
In the old Kentucky state.[24]

Text II

It was one winter evening
The sorrowful tale was told
Scott Jackson said to Walling
Let's take Pearl for a stroll;
Oh, soon the cab was ordered,

[24] "Pearl Bryant," sung by Bascom Lamar Lunsford on Library of Congress recording AAFS 1824B; recorded by Hibbitt and Greet, 1935. Lunsford learned this version from Gilbert (Doc) Tallant, from whom it was collected in 1930 at Asheville, N.C., by Dorothy Scarborough. Tallant's text, which is identical to Lunsford's, is among the unpublished Scarborough mss. at Baylor University, Waco, Texas.

To go out for a stroll
And if you will only listen
The half has never been told.

Pearl went to Cincinnati
She'd never been there before
She said to Sweetheart Jackson
I'll never see Mama no more
She said to Sweetheart Jackson
Why do you want to take my life?
You know I've always loved you
And would have been your wife

Little did Pearl think
When she left her home that day
That the little grip she carried
Would hide her head away
There's room for your name in my album
There's room for your love in my heart
There's room for us both in Heaven
Where true lovers never part

Oh, then some bloodhounds were ordered
They found no trail, they said
Here lies a woman's body
But we can't find no head;
They telephoned for miles around
At last an answer came;
It was from Pearl Bryan's sister
It must be Pearl that's slain.

In came Pearl Bryan's sister
Falling on her knees
A-pleading to Scott Jackson
For sister's head—oh, please!
But Jackson was so stubborn,
A naughty word he said;
When you meet Pearl in Heaven
You'll find her missing head.

In came Walling's mother
A-pleading for her son
A-saying to the jury
    It's the first crime they ever done;
Oh, send him not to prison,
    'Twould break my poor old heart
My son's my darling one,
    How from him can I part?

The jury soon decided
    And from their seat they sprung;
For the crime the boys committed
    They both now must be hung;
On January the thirty-first
    This awful crime was done
Scott Jackson and Alonzo Walling
    Together they were hung.

Oh, boys and girls, take warning,
    Before it is too late;
The worst crime ever committed
    In old Kentucky state.[25]

Pearl Bryan VI

This ballad is, unhappily, even more complicated in its connections with other ballads than is Pearl Bryan V. The earliest date given for it is 1913, if the informant's account is correct.[26]

[25] "The Ballad of Pearl Bryan and Her Sad Death in the Kentucky Hills at Fort Thomas," printed in the Louisville *Courier-Journal*, June 29, 1953. The text comes from a broadside sent to a columnist by Mrs. Verna Jeffers, Whitley City, Ky., who said she had had the broadside since 1932. The columnist reports that beneath the title the broadside indicates an author—"by Frank Jones."

[26] M. E. Henry, in "Notes and Queries," *Journal of American Folklore* 56 (1943): 139, gives the text with the following note: "The following version of 'Pearl Bryan' was communicated by Mrs. Frank Newell, Christie St., Leonia, N.J. who received it from her daughter, Mrs. Marjorie White. She had it from the sister of Mrs. Maud Clark who 'lived out that

This ballad consists of seven verses that wound up in both forms of Pearl Bryan I, one verse that appears both in non-Dalhart I and in V, and four verses plus a two-verse chorus that are not shared with other ballads. This elusive ballad has been collected just twice by itself; once it is blended with I, and in one other case the chorus of VI was used to provide two verses for a conglomerate text. Texts of Pearl Bryan VI collected in 1913 and 1964 include the verses that entered Pearl Bryan I. Once, in either 1949 or 1951, it was collected without any shared verses, but the informant indicated a hiatus in the song.[27]

Internal evidence suggests that the ballad was composed shortly after the crime, for details included in it appear to be from contemporary newspaper accounts. Verse five of the ballad uses the expression "dissecting knife." During the trials of Jackson and Walling, much was made of the bloody scalpel found in Walling's trunk. It was assumed that Jackson and Walling would be particularly adept at cutting off heads because they were in dental training and were, therefore, medical students of a sort. A more impressive instance of dependence on contemporary news accounts is found in the ninth and tenth verses of the model text, which describe a letter written to Will Wood by Scott Jackson. The ballad verses quote the letter almost word for word as it was printed in newspapers during 1896. These verses, and the text of the letter, are given above.

Pearl Bryan VI never achieved great popularity, but it played a seminal role in the development of one of the two main

way where it happened and she sent me [her sister] this copy of the song in November, 1913.' "

[27] Austin Fife, in either 1949 or 1951, recorded a text at Atascadero, Calif., from the singing of Mrs. Effie Carmack. A taped copy of the interview is kept in the Archive of California and Western Folklore, University of California, Los Angeles.

streams of surviving Pearl Bryan balladry. Pearl Bryan I was composed, I think, by taking eight verses from Pearl Bryan VI and adding five newly composed verses. The fact that the uncommon Pearl Bryan VI appears as early as 1913, while the stable and popular Pearl Bryan I appears suddenly in 1927, supports this contention. Further evidence is seen in the circumstantial detail of Pearl Bryan VI that comes directly from newspaper accounts. A model text for Pearl Bryan VI is given below.

> Young ladies, if you listen
> To a story I relate
> That happened near Fort Thomas
> In old Kentucky state,
> It was January 31
> This dreadful deed was done
> By Jackson and Walen to Pearl Bryan.
> How cold their blood must run!

Cho: Poor Pearl! Poor girl,
> She thought she was going right.
> She had no dream of murder
> On that dark stormy night.
> She pled with her executioner
> Pleading was in vain;
> It was the hand of Jackson
> And that was all to blame.

> It was Scott Jackson and Walen
> That took Pearl Bryan's life
> On that dark and stormy night
> With a big detective knife[28]
> Scott Jackson done the planning;
> Walen followed on.

[28] The version collected by Austin Fife, noted in fn. 27, has "dissecting knife" rather than "detective knife"; the latter is no doubt a corruption.

It made the whole world tremble
To see what they had done.

But little did Pearl Bryan think
On that dark and gloomy day
The grip she carried in her hand
Would hide her head away.
She thought it was a lover's hand
She could trust it night and day;
But alas! it was a lover's hand
That hid her head away.

Scott Jackson wrote a letter
To Willis Wood one day;
Told him to write another
To Pearl Bryan's home and say,
"I am not in Indianapolis;
Sign her name, you may;
Stick to your old chum, Bill,
And I'll stick to you some day."

But little did Pearl's parents think
When she left their happy home,
Their darling, dear and sweet,
Would never more return.
The aged parents renew their will.
Their fortune they would give
If Pearly could return again
Another life to live.

Young ladies, now take warning
Since you find young men unjust.
It may be your own best lover's hand;
You know not whom to trust.
Pearl Bryan died away from home
And in that lonely spot.
My God, my God, believe it girls
Don't let this be your lot.[29]

[29] "Pearl Bryan," from Mrs. Marjorie White, Leonia, N.J.; collected by

It has been shown above that all the Pearl Bryan ballads except II have been involved to some degree or other in verse borrowing. Those sharing the fewest verses with other types are Pearl Bryans III and IV; they are also the least popular and apparently the ones most dependent on print for their survival. Pearl Bryan II is both stable and popular. It does share a verse with Pearl Bryan V, but rarely. Pearl Bryan I appears in two versions, both stable and popular, after 1926–1927. It is argued that the few Pearl Bryan I verses found before this date belong to Pearl Bryan VI, which is to some degree a proto–Pearl Bryan I. Pearl Bryan I, I think, is based on a number of verses from Pearl Bryan VI. It is probable that Pearl Bryan V also borrowed from Pearl Bryan VI. If this is the case, Pearl Bryan VI may be one of the oldest Pearl Bryan ballads. Certainly Pearl Bryans II, V, and VI are older than Pearl Bryan I, for all are attested before 1926–1927.

The history of the relationship of these six ballads, incomplete as it is, does show to some degree the ascendance of the murdered-girl pattern over the criminal-brought-to-justice pattern. For example, Pearl Bryan VI contains four verses that describe in detail the criminal's plans and actions and his schemes for evading justice. He, the actor, is the center of attention, not the passive victim. In this it follows the criminal pattern. These verses are omitted by Pearl Bryan I in its selection of verses from Pearl Bryan VI. Those which it chooses suit the murdered-girl pattern, which Pearl Bryan I follows. Pearl Bryan V borrows a verse shared by Pearl Bryans I and VI, which describes how little Pearl wot that her grip was destined to carry her head. In its concentration on the pathos of the murdered girl rather than on the woeful end of the criminal, this verse follows the

M. E. Henry and printed in *Journal of American Folklore* 56 (1943): 139. See fn. 26 above.

murdered-girl rather than the criminal-brought-to-justice formula. Although Pearl Bryan V has strong elements of the criminal formula, this verse is definitely in the murdered-girl tradition; hence this borrowing also shows the direction in which all the Pearl Bryan ballads move. The pair of verses that Pearl Bryan V borrows from II (the "what-have-I-done" and the "album" verses described above) are also of the murdered-girl type. Pearl Bryan II follows the murdered-girl pattern from the beginning, with some small adjustments for the facts of the case in the earlier texts. In the next section, however, it will be seen that internal details in Pearl Bryan II also change over time toward greater agreement with the formula.

INTERNAL HISTORY OF THE BALLADS

So far we have considered the genealogy of the ballads—how their interrelationship affected their development. This section considers the internal history of each type, showing what changes, if any, have come with time.

Pearl Bryan I, as noted above, appeared rather suddenly around 1926–1927. This ballad has been quite stable, but it shows some slight changes of interest. These changes occur only in the non-Dalhart stream of texts. Those which follow the Dalhart pattern suffer almost no changes. The non-Dalhart stream shows a tendency to blend the two murderers into one, called variously "Jackson Waldon," "Jack Walling," or "Jackson and by wailing." At other times it tends to garble the names, for instance, "Wall and Jackson," or "Jackson and Wallace." Before 1940, the names are confused in two out of four non-Dalhart texts; after 1940, the names are confused in seven out of eight non-Dalhart texts.

Pearl Bryan II shows some rather interesting developments over time. In its earlier forms it often clung to the facts and named both murderers:

> Down to poor Pearl's dwelling
> Jackson and Walling flew

As time passed, Walling disappeared and Jackson became sole murderer. In four cases, the lover has no name at all. Before 1927, Jackson and Walling both, or a corruption blending the two, such as "Jackson Walton," appear in seven out of a total of twenty-four texts. Between 1928 and 1938, such a form appears only once. After 1938, Walling disappears entirely. Of the post-1938 texts, twenty-five out of thirty-two name Jackson only as lover-murderer, four give him no name, two call him "Edward," and one calls him "Dustin."[30]

Another development in Pearl Bryan II is the gradual disappearance of any reference to decapitation. Headlessness appears in eleven out of twenty-four texts up to 1927, in two out of seven between 1928 and 1938, and not at all after 1938.

Pearl Bryan V has not shown much change in its formulae. One would expect that the murdered-girl verses would tend to crowd out the criminal-brought-to-justice verses, but this cannot be shown clearly except in the case of fragments or abbreviated versions. The fragments do tend to preserve murdered-girl verses more than criminal ones. However, the verses that Pearl Bryan V borrowed from II and VI were of the murdered-girl type rather than the criminal type, as outlined above.

Pearl Bryan V appears to be dying out, although the verses describing the plea for the missing head go on as borrowed items in other ballads. Since 1940, Pearl Bryan V has appeared three times, only once as a complete version. In the other two cases the plea-for-head element, but little else, is preserved and tacked onto another song. The plea for the head, although parallel in construction to Mrs. Walling's plea for her son's life, is in content murdered-girl rather than criminal-brought-to-jus-

[30] "Dustin" may be derived from "Dusty," which was, in fact, Scott Jackson's nickname.

tice. The grieving parents of the girl belong to the murdered-girl formula; grieving parents of the criminal belong to the criminal pattern. The popularity of the plea for the head as a borrowed item shows that, when a native American rhapsode is stitching together a ballad about Pearl Bryan, elements of the murdered-girl pattern are considered more appropriate than elements of the criminal-brought-to-justice pattern.

The similarity between news and ballad formulae extends beyond the progressive ascendance of the murdered-girl plot formula. The two also share formulaic epithets, characterization, and action sequences. These are treated below.

Epithets

In Chapter 2 it was noted that in newspapers the word "aged" almost invariably accompanied the word "parent" if the parents designated were those of Pearl Bryan, Scott Jackson, and Alonzo Walling. This is a favored locution in American vulgar balladry generally, although it occurs in only two of the six Pearl Bryan ballads. Pearl Bryan VI and Pearl Bryan I often share the following verse:

> Her aged parents we all know
> Their fortune they would give
> If Pearl again returned to them
> Her natural life to live

An expression used frequently by both newspapers and ballads is "poor Pearl Bryan" and what might be considered its variants, "poor girl" and "poor Pearl." Here are some newspaper examples:

"Just where this snow lies," said Mr. Locke, "is where poor Pearl's head would have rested had the brutal murderers left it."[31]

[31] *Star-Press* (Greencastle), February 15, 1896.

"I ask you, Scott Jackson," and the woman's voice sounded out plain and distinct in the deadly quiet that prevailed, "to tell me what you have done with poor Pearl's head."[32]

It is believed by most people here that Wood is to blame for the poor girl's downfall . . .[33]

The return of the headless body of poor Pearl Bryan is likely to produce the greatest excitement ever known here.[34]

SCIENTIFIC READINGS
Of the Characters of Jackson, Walling, and Poor Pearl Bryan[35]

Four of the six ballads of Pearl Bryan use the epithets "poor Pearl Bryan," "poor Pearl," and "poor girl." The union of "poor" and "Pearl" is almost as fixed as that of "aged" and "parent." Texts of Pearl Bryan I contain the epithet in the following verses:

> The driver was the only one
> Could tell her awful fate
> Of poor Pearl far away from home
> In old Kentucky state

> The driver Jackson tells the story
> How poor Pearl Bryan did moan
> From Cincinnati to the place
> Where the dreadful deed was done

> Pearl's aged parents we know well
> A fortune they would give
> If poor Pearl had again returned to home
> A natural life to live

[32] Ibid.
[33] *Evening Democrat* (Greencastle), February 15, 1896.
[34] *Enquirer* (Cincinnati), February 9, 1896.
[35] Ibid., a headline.

> It was January thirty-first
> This dreadful deed was done
> By Jackson and by Walling
> How poor Pearl's blood did run!

Pearl Bryan II is an adaptation of "The Jealous Lover" and usually uses the epithets common to that form. The heroine of "The Jealous Lover" is, variously, Florella, Lorilla, Flow-Ella, and so on, and never has the adjective "poor" attached to her name. Her usual epithet is "own" or "sweet," as in the following lines:

> Way down in the lonely valley
> Where the violets fade and bloom
> 'Tis there my sweet [own] Lorella [Florella, etc.]
> Lies mouldering in the tomb

Thus, normally the Pearl Bryan adaptations run:

> Our own [sweet] Pearl Bryan slumbers
> In a cold and silent tomb

However, "poor Pearl" finds its way into twelve texts of Pearl Bryan II, in such verses as the following:

> Down in a lonely valley
> Where the fairest flowers bloom
> There's where poor Pearl Bryan
> Lies mouldering in her tomb

> White banner floating o'er her
> Her thrills in triumph sound
> A stranger found poor Pearl
> Lying cold, headless, on the ground

Pearl Bryans IV and VI normally use this epithet, as will be seen from an examination of the model texts. Pearl Bryan III does not usually contain it; but, of the six collected texts, one shows intrusion of the form "poor Pearl" in the following verse:

> In a cab one rainy evening
> At the close of one sad day
> When Lon Walling and Scott Jackson
> Came and took poor Pearl away.[36]

Pearl Bryan V does not normally contain this epithet. As in the case of Pearl Bryan II, there is one exception; here it is a text that interpolates the epithet three times into the song, in the following verses:

> The message was brought back to her home
> That poor Pearl Bryan was dead
> Killed by Wollen and by Jackson
> And they took away her head
>
> In came poor Pearl's mother
> And turning to Jackson said
> You have killed my daughter
> Please tell me where's her head
>
> On that cold cold winter morning
> The people for miles around said
> We've found a poor girl's body
> But we can not find her head[37]

"The missing head" was an expression appearing occasionally in newspapers that made its way into a popular verse of Pearl Bryan V:

> She turned away in tears
> And wept aloud and said
> When I meet my sister in heaven
> I'll find the missing head

[36] "Pearl Bryon," from Olive C. Kay, Evans, W.Va., June 1927. In Robert W. Gordon, unpublished mss. at the Library of Congress, Washington, D.C.

[37] From Doc Hopkins, Los Angeles, Calif., June 1965; the text was contained in a letter to the author.

Chapter 2 reported some of the many epithets used in newspapers for the parents of Jackson, Walling, and Pearl Bryan. "Afflicted father and mother," "unfortunate families," "suffering sister," and "grief-stricken parents" are examples of expressions used. The ballads have a more limited repertoire. Usually, no epithet accompanies a character. "In come Pearl Bryan's sister" or "It was Scott and Walling that took Pearl Bryan's life" are examples of how characters are introduced in the ballads—they simply appear, performing the actions assigned to them. Three parental epithets appear in the Pearl Bryan ballads. Pearl Bryan I uses either "dear old parents" or "aged parents," while Pearl Bryan II uses "loving parents."

For the crime itself the newspapers had a variety of descriptive names, among them the following: "The Fort Thomas horror," "the Fort Thomas tragedy," "the awful crime," "the horrid crime," "the horrible crime," "the terrible crime," "the crime of the century," "the foul deed," "the dreadful deed," "the devilish deed," "the cruel murder," and, simply, "the Pearl Bryan murder." The most popular of these expressions were "the Fort Thomas horror" and "the horrible crime," although "the Fort Thomas tragedy" and "the awful crime" were also common.

Of the ballads only Pearl Bryans I and VI use such expressions for the crime. Pearl Bryan VI uses "dreadful deed" and "awful deed." The Dalhart versions of Pearl Bryan I have three expressions for the murder: "awful deed," "cruel deed," and "awful fate." The non-Dalhart versions use "dreadful fate," "sad fate," "dreadful deed," "awful deed," "terrible deed," "lawless deed," "lonesome deed," "lowly deed," and "lowest deed." The last four in this list all appear to be variations of one original form, probably "lawless deed."

The only expressions for the crime I found shared by newspapers and ballads were "awful deed" and "dreadful deed." The only nouns used by the ballads in their limited repertoire of epithets were "deed" and "fate." The newspapers used many nouns, but the most common were "horror" (used only in the expression "the Fort Thomas horror") and "crime" (used with a variety of adjectives). As for the adjectival half of the epithet, there is more agreement. Both newspaper and ballad commonly used "awful," and they also shared "dreadful," "terrible," and "cruel."

There are other cases where sequences of words appearing in newspaper stories have exact echoes in the ballads. If there is anything more in these than coincidence, it is simply similarity in style. But I note them as items of interest. In the Greencastle *Evening Democrat* the following sentence appears: "He drove out to the residence of A. S. Bryan in the afternoon to get some letters to use in the prosecution of Wm. Trusty, the fellow who swore that he drove a wagon containing Pearl Bryan's body from Cincinnati to the place where it was found."[38] The phrase "from Cincinnati to the place where" is repeated in the following verse from Pearl Bryan I:

> The driver Jackson tells the tale
> Of how the girl did moan
> From Cincinnati to the place
> Where the dreadful deed was done

A similar locution was used by the Louisville *Evening Post*: "Arrived near Fort Thomas, the girl was taken from the vehicle and to the spot where her body was found."[39]

Another interesting example of the same idea appearing in both newspapers and ballads is found in the following passages. First, from the Greencastle *Evening Democrat*: ". . . these three fiends are as certainly guilty as the sun rises and sets."[40]

[38] *Evening Democrat* (Greencastle), September 28, 1896.
[39] *Evening Post* (Louisville), February 8, 1896.
[40] *Evening Democrat* (Greencastle), February 15, 1896.

And from Pearl Bryan II:

> Down on his knees he bended
> Crying "Oh, what have I done"
> I've murdered blue eyed Pearl
> As sure as the rising sun[41]

The last example of similar or identical phrasing is the following from the Louisville *Evening Post*: "She [Pearl] told me what had happened and said that Jackson was to blame"[42] and from Pearl Bryan VI:

> She pled with her executioner
> Pleading was in vain
> It was the hand of Jackson
> And that was all to blame

STEREOTYPED CHARACTERS

Chapter 2 discussed the stereotyped roles assigned by the newspapers to the principals in the Pearl Bryan case and showed that these principals were perceived in terms of particular stereotypes even when their actions suggested the stereotypes were inappropriate. These roles carry out the action in the ballads as well. Basically, there are three roles: the Mur-

[41] This verse, which appears also in "The Jealous Lover," may be a very old one in Anglo-American folk poetry. Marie Campbell, in "Survivals of Old Folk Drama in the Kentucky Mountains," *Journal of American Folklore* 51 (1938): 10–24, gives three examples of similar verses used in folk drama. The first two come from a mummers' play given in 1930, and the third from two informants' memories of a Plough Monday Play:

Old Father Christmas	I cut her down
See what you've done	Like the evening sun
You've bloody killed	
Your own loved one	What have you done?
	Killed the best woman
Horrible, terrible	Under the sun
See what I've done	

[42] *Evening Post* (Louisville), February 8, 1896.

dered Girl, the Lover-Murderer, and the Grief-Stricken Families.

The Murdered Girl

According to the stereotype, the victim of the murder must be young, trusting, and innocent. She must be helpless vis-à-vis her betrayer. She is greatly attached to her home and family, where she is cherished. To some extent her character is revealed in the few epithets for her found in the ballads: she was a "young girl," a "fair young maiden"; she was "young and gay"; she was also "poor Pearl" and her parents' "darling girl."

Her character is expressed not so much in epithets as in what she does and what happens to her. Her trusting innocence is shown in such lines as the following from Pearl Bryan I:

> And little did Pearl Bryan think
> When she left her happy home
> The grip she carried in her hand
> Would hide her head away
>
> She thought it was a lover's hand
> That she could trust each day
> Alas, it was a lover's hand
> That took her life away

Her excess of confidence is implied in these lines:

> Young ladies now take warning
> Young men are so unjust
> It may be your best lover
> But you know not whom to trust

When Jackson threatens Pearl, Pearl Bryan V has her answer with undiminished love, as in Pearl Bryan II:

> Oh what have I done, Scott Jackson
> For you to take my life?
> You know I always loved you
> And would of been your wife

Pearl Bryan VI also describes Pearl's fatal confidence:

> Poor Pearl, poor Pearl, she tried to save her life
> She had no dream of murder until she saw the knife

An alternative version is:

> Poor Pearl! Poor girl
> She thought she was going right
> She had no dream of murder
> On that dark stormy night

Pearl's helplessness in respect to Jackson is always stressed.
From Pearl Bryan I:

> How bold these cruel villains
> To do this awful deed
> To hide away Pearl Bryan
> When she to them did plead
>
> The driver tells the story
> Of how Pearl Bryan did moan
> From Cincinnati to the place
> Where the cruel deed was done
>
> How sad it must have been for him
> To hear Pearl's pleading voice
> At midnight in the lonely spot
> Where those two men rejoiced

From Pearl Bryan II:

> Oh Jackson I am weary
> Of us roaming here alone
> The way 'tis cold and dreary
> I pray you take me home
>
> Now Pearl I have you
> You have no wings to fly
> No mortal arms can reach you
> Now Pearl, you must die

> Down on her knees she bended
> Pleading for her life
> But in her snow white bosom
> He plunged the fatal knife

Pearl Bryan III expresses the idea succinctly:

> Yes, they took her from this city
> Far away from friends and home
> And they left her body lying
> Headless, bloodstained, all alone

In a different way, Pearl Bryan IV shows Pearl's helplessness in respect to Jackson. She is shown pleading with him to legitimize her baby, but he refuses and heartlessly abandons her. She follows him, and he murders her. She is unable either to pressure him into giving her respectability, or even to preserve her life once he is angered.

> The maiden soon of him did plead a great wrong for to right
> "I thought now you will not, dearest, leave me in my present plight."
> He only smiled and answered her, "Young girl, you loved too true,
> I leave you now, farewell, we part, adieu, part, love, adieu."
>
> Rather than face her many friends, she followed in his path
> He led her to a lonely spot, and awful was his wrath;
> But little did he think that far above in the blue sky
> A witness there who sees a crime with an all-seeing eye.

Pearl Bryan V describes Pearl's passiveness and misery:

> The cab then arriving
> Pearl Bryan sat in tears
> Thinking of the happiness
> She had had in the last few years

> Pearl went to Cincinnata
> She had not been there before
> She was led astray by Scott Jackson
> To never see Mama no more

Pearl Bryan VI also describes Pearl's weakness in respect to her murderer:

> She pled with her executioner
> Pleading was in vain
> It was the hand of Jackson
> And that was all to blame

In the verses cited, most of the action is done to or upon Pearl. She is "taken" for a ride, and she is "led" astray. True, she "goes" to Cincinnati, but the qualifying clause "she had not been there before" suggests her helplessness and bewilderment in a strange city. The other action she performs in these verses is to "sit in tears."

The attachment between the murdered girl and her family is expressed in almost all the ballads. From Pearl Bryan I:

> Little did Pearl's parents think
> When she left her happy home
> Their darling girl in her youth
> Would nevermore return
>
> Her aged parents we all know
> Their fortune they would give
> If Pearl again returned to them
> Her natural life to live

From Pearl Bryan II:

> Farewell my loving parents
> My face you'll never see more
> Long long you'll wait my coming
> To the little cottage door

> Farewell my darling sister
> My peaceful, happy home
> Farewell my dear old schoolmates
> With you no more I'll roam

From Pearl Bryan IV:

> In Greencastle, Indiana, a fair young maiden dwelled
> Beneath a mother's loving care, a father's lavish wealth
> A mother's pride, a father's joy by many friends
> esteemed
> From out of her young handsome face the pure
> innocence gleamed.

From Pearl Bryan V:

> She was led astray by Scott Jackson
> To never see Mama no more
>
> In came Pearlie's sister
> Fell down on her knees
> Pleading to Jackson
> Give sister's head, oh please

Pearl Bryan VI contains the same verses on this subject as Pearl Bryan I, which are given above.

The Lover-Murderer

Scott Jackson, established as principal murderer, was portrayed in the newspapers as cold, calculating, brutal, clever, conscienceless, and as a man of action and daring. His only saving virtue was a real concern for his mother. Walling, once he was established as secondary murderer, was portrayed as weak and dull and tending toward vice. He was usually described as the tool of Jackson or as being under Jackson's influence. His relations with his family were seen as close, and his mother's efforts to save him aroused considerable sympathy. For the most part, the ballads portray the two men in much the same manner as did the newspapers. Jackson's cleverness is seen in the fact that he tricks Pearl to her doom and in the frequent statement that he did all the planning for the deed. Some sample lines will show this characteristic. From Pearl Bryan I:

> She thought it was a lover's hand
> That she could trust each day
> Alas, it was a lover's hand
> That took her life away

From Pearl Bryan II:

> Come Pearl, let's take a ramble
> Through meadows sweet and gay
> Where no one can disturb us
> We'll name our wedding day
>
> .   .   .   .
>
> Down in these woods I have you
> From me you cannot fly
> No human arms can save you
> Pearl Bryan you must die

From Pearl Bryan V:

> Scott Jackson says to Waldon
> Says to him by his side
> Pearl Bright she's a fair young lady
> Let's take her out for a ride

From Pearl Bryan VI:

> Jackson did the planning
> And Walling followed on
> It made the whole world tremble
> To think of what they had done
>
> .   .   .   .

> Scott Jackson wrote a letter
> To Willis Wood one day
> Told him to write another
> To Pearl Bryan's home and say
>
> "I am not in Indianapolis"
> Sign her name you may;
> Stick to your old chum, Bill,
> And I'll stick to you some day

Jackson's coldness and brutality are shown in the form of the murder itself—beheading his victim. Sometimes there are editorial remarks on this characteristic:

> How bolden were those wicked men
> To do this lonesome deed
> To hide away Pearl Bryan's head
> When she to them did plead

> The evidence does plainly implicate all three of them
> For more atrocious crime no man did ever hang

> Oh boys and girls take warning
> Before it is too late
> The worst crime ever committed
> In old Kentucky State

Walling usually appears in the ballads as a secondary figure, a position he filled in newspaper stories as well. When he is composed into the ballad as a figure equally guilty with Jackson, there is a tendency to forget him as the ballad is shaped by time. For example, in Pearl Bryan I the second verse usually runs:

> On January the thirty-first
> The dreadful deed was done
> By Jackson and by Walling
> How cold their blood did run

The last two lines, however, are sometimes modified to such
forms as:

> By Jackson and by wailing
> How cold Pearl's blood did run

> By Jack Walling and Pearl Bryon
> How cold their blood did run

> By Jackson Waldon and Pearl Bryan
> How cold their blood must run

In other cases, Walling's name is distorted:

> By Wall and by Jackson
> How cold the blood must run

> By Jackson and Wallace
> How cold their blood did run

Pearl Bryan IV, written apparently before the first trial in the
case was over, tells the entire story of Pearl's betrayal and
murder, with Scott Jackson as both lover and murderer. In its
penultimate stanza it seems suddenly recalled to reality and
makes an announcement introducing two new characters: "The
evidence does plainly implicate all three of them . . . Scott
Jackson, Alonza Walling, and Will Wood."

Pearl Bryan II usually ignores Walling altogether and names
only Scott Jackson as lover-murderer. Some of the earlier texts
are more compelled by the historical facts and begin by naming
both men:

> Down to poor Pearl's dwelling
> Jackson and Walling flew

After a few lines the pressure of the murdered-girl formula
is too strong, and Walling is abandoned. Thus, as soon as Pearl
is induced to take the fatal stroll the number of dramatis per-

sonae returns to the usual two, and it is to Jackson alone that
Pearl makes her plea for her life.

In Pearl Bryan III Walling's role is a little unusual. The story
of Pearl's ruin by Scott Jackson and Jackson's consternation
when he learns Pearl is pregnant is told. After a moment's
doubt, Jackson decides what to do:

> Then he called on his friend Walling
> For to seek advice and aid
> And they held a consultation
> Where this dying plot was made

Walling enters the story as an equal partner in crime with
Jackson. The tale ends with the statement, "they killed her,
surely killed her," and no mention of retribution is made.

Pearl Bryan V wavers somewhat between two murderers
and one. Scott Jackson initiates the fatal plan, saying to
Walling:

> Pearl Bright she's a fair young lady
> Let's take her out for a ride

Arrived, apparently, at their destination, Pearl then makes the
usual Pearl Bryan II plea, which is to Jackson only:

> Oh what have I done, Scott Jackson
> That you should take my life?
> You know I always loved you
> And would have been your wife

After the body is identified, Pearl's sister comes to make her
plea, also to Jackson only:

> In came Pearl Bryan's sister
> To falling on her knees
> A-pleading with Scott Jackson
> Her sister's head, oh please

Walling is not forgotten, however, because

> In came Lonz Wallon's mother
> A-pleading for her son
> A-pleading to the jurors
> For the first crime he'd ever done

At the end, the ballad has it that both men are guilty:

> So now young ladies take warning
> Before it is too late
> Of the crime that the boys committed
> In the old Kentucky state

Pearl Bryan VI states:

> It was Scott and Walling
> That took Pearl Bryan's life

but their roles in the crime are different.

> Jackson did the planning
> And Walling followed on

Like Pearl Bryan V, it wavers between the legal facts—both men were convicted—and the murdered-girl formula—the lover and the murderer are one and the same. For, in another verse, Pearl Bryan VI states:

> She pled with her executioner
> Pleading was in vain
> It was the hand of Jackson
> And that was all to blame

Grief-Stricken Families

The parents of Pearl Bryan, Scott Jackson, and Alonzo Walling were portrayed as grief-stricken and careworn by events, devoted to their children, but helpless to alter their unhappy fates. Particular notice is given the mothers.

Pearl Bryan I tells of the pathetic and unavailing wishes of Pearl's parents:

> Her parents we know well
> Their fortune they would give
> If Pearl would just return home
> Her natural life to live

A recently recorded rewrite that takes most of its elements from Pearl Bryan I introduces and expands from Pearl Bryan V one of the pleading verses; but here Pearl's parents are in the kneeling position usually assumed by her sister:

> Pearl Bryon's loving parents
> Fell down on their knees
> They pleaded with Scott Jackson
> Please Scott, oh tell us please
>
> Why did you kill our daughter
> Pearl didn't want to die
> She loved you so, Scott Jackson
> Please tell us, tell us why[43]

Two other versions of Pearl Bryan I that tack on elements from Pearl Bryan V include parental pleading. A version recorded about 1964 also changes Pearl's sister into a parent:

> Then in came poor Pearl's mother
> And turning to Jackson said
> You have killed my daughter Pearl
> Please tell me where's her head[44]

A 1935 text of I adds verses from V in more conventional form. It is Pearl's sister who pleads for the head, and the pleading mother is Walling's mother:

[43] Nevada Slim (Rev. Dallas Turner), "Pearl Bryon," Rural Rhythm RRNS 166 A 67 (1967).

[44] The Phipps Family, "Pearl Bryan," Folkways FA 2375 (1964?).

> In came Walling's mother
> Pleading for her son
>
> .   .   .   .
> .   .   .   .
>
> Don't take my son, my only son
> From him I cannot part
> O please don't take him to prison
> It would break my poor old heart[45]

Pearl Bryan II is interested almost exclusively in the inter-action between Pearl and Scott Jackson, but in her dying speech Pearl assigns the usual passively sorrowful role to her parents:

> Farewell dear loving parents
> My face you'll see no more
> You'll long and wait my coming
> To the lone little cottage door

Pearl Bryan IV emphasizes the devotion of Pearl's parents to her while she is alive, but, since the ballad ends with her mur-der and a moral, there is no place for the grief-stricken parents to enter the stage.

Pearl Bryan V originated the much-borrowed verse in which Pearl Bryan's sister, on her knees, begs Jackson for Pearl's head and the verse in which Walling's mother pleads to the jury for her son. In some versions, the absence of a sorrowing parent for Pearl is remedied. In a 1937 text, both Pearl's sister and her mother plead with Jackson:

> Oh, in come Pearl Bryan's mother
> She fell to her knees and said
> Oh you have killed my daughter
> Please tell me where she is

---

45 Paul Brewster, "A" Text, *Ballads and Songs of Indiana*, pp. 283–285.

> *Chorus*: Please tell me where she is
> Please tell me where she is
> Oh you have killed my daughter Pearl
> Please tell me where she is
>
> Oh in come Pearl Bryan's sister
> A-turning to Jackson she said
> Oh you have killed my sister Pearl
> Please tell me where's her head
>
> *Chorus*: Please tell me where's her head[46]

. . . .

In this text the sorrowing families do a great deal of pleading, especially as the last two lines of each verse are made into a chorus. In this text we have the only appearance of Jackson's mother, taking over Mrs. Walling's plea to the jury:

> Oh in come Jackson's mother
> A-pleading for her son
> Saying gentlemen of this jury
> 'Tis the first crime they have done
>
> *Chorus*: 'Tis the first crime they have done

. . . .

A 1930 text includes a sorrowing-family verse found also in Pearl Bryans VI and I:

> Pearlie's parents now in sorrow
> Their fortune they give
> If their darling girl could come back
> To them—her natural life to live[47]

---

[46] "Pearl Bryant," from Ellie D. Sibert, Clay Co., Ky., 1937; collected by Alan and Elizabeth Lomax and deposited in the Library of Congress, available on AAFS 1477A.

[47] "Pearlie Bryant," from Miss Rachel Tucker, Varnell, Ga., 1930; in M. E. Henry, "Still More Ballads and Folk-Songs from the Southern Highlands," *Journal of American Folklore* 45 (1932): 132–134.

Pearl Bryan VI expresses the devotion and misery of Pearl's parents in the same verses noted for Pearl Bryan I.

It may be wondered why, with but one exception, only Pearl Bryan's and Walling's parents appear in the ballads. This is due to a combination of historic circumstance and formulaic composition. Mrs. Walling did indeed make highly publicized appeals for her son, once to the Bryan family and once to Governor Bradley of Kentucky. Both were unavailing. While the Jackson family through lawyers appealed to the governor for clemency, this effort did not receive the sympathy or publicity of Mrs. Walling's activity. Mrs. Walling's appearance in the ballads, therefore, has some historical foundation; but the presentation (or lack thereof) of parental figures in the ballads is primarily a formulaic one. Pearl's parents appear passive and grieving because that is what the murdered-girl's parents must do. Mrs. Jackson does not appear, because the lover-murderer's parents do not appear. Mrs. Walling's presence is in connection with the criminal-brought-to-justice formula, where it is standard for the criminal's parents to plead to the bar. Note that Mrs. Walling's unusual and highly dramatic plea to Pearl's parents is omitted in the ballads, whereas her legally routine appeal for executive clemency has been transformed into an appeal to the judge and jury, a standard element of the criminal-brought-to-justice formula.

SCENE FORMULAE

Certain scenes are familiar to every reader or hearer of American vulgar balladry. In ballads of the criminal-brought-to-justice type there is a courtroom scene, where either the criminal himself or one of his parents pleads for his life or liberty; there is a visit in prison, where the criminal's relatives come to weep over him; or there is a scaffold scene where the criminal makes his farewell. In ballads of the murdered-girl type there is a luring scene, in which the lover entices the girl away to a lonely spot; there is a murder scene, in which the girl pleads on bended knee for her life; there is an abandoned-body scene, in which the body is described in its setting; sometimes there is a regret scene, in which the murderer deplores his deed.

Pearl Bryan I has scenes only of the murdered-girl type. The luring scene is given in the following words:

> The driver Jackson tells the story
> How poor Pearl Bryon did moan
> From Cincinnati to the place
> Where the dreadful deed was done

The pleading scene is mentioned twice:

> How sad it must have been for him
> To hear Pearl's pleading voice
> At midnight in the lonely spot
> Where those two men rejoiced

> How bold those wretched men must be
> To do this dreadful deed
> To hide away Pearl Bryan's head
> When she to them did plead

The abandoned-body scene is given:

> Next day a farmer passing by
> Spied a lifeless form
> A-lying on the cold damp ground
> And the blood stained all around

Pearl Bryan II also has scenes of the murdered-girl type only. Several verses are devoted to the luring scene:

> Come, Pearl, come let's go wander
> In the meadows deep and gay

Where no disturber shall ponder
We'll name our wedding day

Deep, deep down in the valley
He led his love so dear
She said "'Tis for you only
That I have wandered here

The way is dark and dreary
And I'm afraid to stay
Of rambling I've grown weary
And I would retrace my way"

At this point Scott Jackson reveals his terrible purpose, and we proceed to the murder scene:

Retrace your way, no never
These woods no more you'll roam
Now bid farewell forever
To parents, friends, and home

Down on her knees before him
She pleaded for her life
But deep into her bosom
He plunged the fatal knife

Pearl then makes a speech bidding her friends and relatives farewell and assigns her parents the melancholy task of waiting forever for her at their cabin door. Frequently she forgives Jackson with her dying breath. Following this is the abandoned-body scene:

The birds sang in the morning
Their awful, weary song
They found Pearl Bryan lying
Upon the cold cold ground

In four texts Pearl Bryan II displays a regret scene. Three are of the following form:

> Down on his knees he bended
> Saying, oh what have I done
> I've murdered my Pearl Bryan
> As pure as the rising sun[48]

A fourth shows the murderer's regret in this fashion:

> Today I'm sad and lonely
> For she was to have been my bride
> But instead of that she's sleeping
> Down by yon river side[49]

Pearl Bryan III opens with a description of how Pearl Bryan was led astray by Scott Jackson. Then it moves to the luring scene:

> In a cab one rainy evening
> At the closing of the day
> Up drove Walling and Scott Jackson
> And with Pearl they drove away
>
> This young girl with all her beauty
> Left the city with these men
> Little did she think that moment
> What would be her woeful end

The murder scene is omitted, but the abandoned body is described:

> Yes, they took her from this city
> Far away from friends and home

---

[48] "Pearl Bryan," from Mrs. Martha Quick, Linn, Mo., 1966, in text sent to author; "Pearl Bryan," from Frances Ollender, Alton, W.Va., 1927, in Robert W. Gordon, unpublished mss. at Library of Congress, Washington, D.C.; "Pearl Bryan," from Bradley Kincaid, *My Favorite Mountain Ballads and Old-Time Songs*, 1928.

[49] "Ballad of 'Pearl Bryan'," from Mrs. F. W. Billings, Dalton, Mass., ca. 1925, in Robert W. Gordon, unpublished mss. at Library of Congress, Washington, D.C.

> And they left her body lying
> Headless, bloodstain, all alone

Pearl Bryan IV, like Pearl Bryan III, devotes its opening verses to Pearl's ruin. The luring and murder are encompassed in one line:

> He led her to a lonely spot, and awful was his wrath

One more line describes the abandoned body:

> All night a headless body lay aside a lonely street

Both Pearl Bryan III and Pearl Bryan IV, the least popular of the six ballads considered here, deviate somewhat from the murdered-girl pattern by expanding upon Pearl's sexual ruin by Scott Jackson and giving short shrift to the details of her murder. The great popularity of I and II, which focus upon the murder scene itself, suggests that this scene is the central feature of the pattern.

In Pearl Bryan V we find a combination of murdered-girl and criminal scenes. The ballad begins with a luring scene:

> Scott Jackson says to Waldon
> Says to him by his side
> Pearl Bright she's a fair young lady
> Let's take her out for a ride

> The cab then arriving
> Pearl Bryant sat in tears
> Thinking of the happiness
> She had had in the last few years

The murder scene is given through Pearl's speech to Jackson at the fatal spot:

> Oh what have I done, Scott Jackson
> For you to take my life?
> You know I always loved you
> And would of been your wife

This intrusion from Pearl Bryan II may have been inserted to fill the gap left by omission of a murder scene in the earlier form of Pearl Bryan V. The earliest text does not have this verse and presents the murder in the following verse only:

> A cab then was ordered
> To take her for a ride
> Oh, if you'll only listen now
> I will tell you how she died

Once Pearl's murder is accomplished, the ballad shifts from the murdered-girl formula to the criminal-brought-to-justice formula. The pursuit of the criminal is given in the following lines:

> Oh then some bloodhounds were ordered
> They found no trail, they said
> Here lies a woman's body
> But we can't find no head

The courtroom scene is given:

> In come Wallon's mother
> Pleading for her son
> Saying unto the jury
> 'Tis the first crime he has done
>
> Oh do not send him to prison
> For it'd break my poor old heart
> For he's my son, my only son
> How can I from him depart

The Law answers as the Law always does in such scenes:

> The jury gave one answer
> Upon their feet they sprang
> The crime these boys committed
> They both will have to hang

The prison-visit scene, found in other criminal-brought-to-justice ballads, does not appear in Pearl Bryan V. The scaffold scene is also missing, except by implication in a line frequently found in the ballad:

> Jackson and Walling's hung

or

> Together they were hung

One text, a pastiche of verses from three Pearl Bryan ballads, held together with the chorus from the popular song "The Band Played On," does add a hanging scene:

> Now they stepped on the scaffold at morning
> Standing there side by side
> Said Walling to Jackson
> You could save my life if you would[50]

Pearl Bryan VI is primarily of the murdered-girl type and contains the standard murdered-girl scenes. The luring is expressed indirectly in an editorial exclamation describing Pearl's lack of caution as she accompanied Jackson:

> Poor Pearl! poor girl
> She thought she was going right
> She had no dream of murder
> On that dark stormy night

The murder scene takes two verses:

> She pled with her executioner
> Pleading was in vain
> It was the hand of Jackson
> And that was all to blame

---

[50] Forrest Lewis, Parksville, Ky., 1958. From unpublished field recording made by Ed Kahn.

It was Scott Jackson and Walen
That took Pearl Bryan's life
On that dark stormy night
With a big detective knife

The abandoned-body scene does not appear in this ballad.

There are twelve lines in this ballad that I would class as a part of the criminal pattern:

Scott Jackson done the planning
Walen followed on
It made the whole world tremble
To see what they had done

. . . .

Scott Jackson wrote a letter
To Willis Wood one day
Told him to write another
To Pearl Bryon's home and say
"I am not in Indianapolis"
Sign her name, you may
Stick to your old chum, Bill
And I'll stick to you some day

These lines indicate the criminal's additional crime (accomplice in forgery) in his attempt to evade capture. The murdered-girl pattern revolves around but one event, the murder of the girl. Association with bad companions, escape, and capture are part of the criminal pattern.

4. CONCLUSION

SHEATHED
Is Justice's Sword
Pearl Bryan's Foul Murder
Is Avenged
End of the Greatest Tragedy of
the Century

The preceding chapters have tried to show how stereotypes, models, or formulae affect interpretation of events. The documents examined for these stereotypes were newspaper and ballad versions of the same historical event. It was seen that a number of formulae appeared in both newspaper and ballad accounts. These formulae were of several types: stock plots, stock scenes, stock characters, and stock sequences of words. In addition, both media employed a stock dramatic device, the "plea-refusal sequence," which will be discussed below.

The newspapers presented the story of Pearl Bryan in terms of two plot formulae familiar to American balladry, which are called here "the murdered-girl formula" and "the criminal-brought-to-justice formula." Each plot formula consists of a standard series of events. The events of the murdered-girl formula are the following: wooing of trusting girl by artful man;

luring of girl to lonely spot; murder of girl, who offers little resistance; abandonment of girl's body. Occasionally a fifth element—regret—is added, in which the murderer is sorry for
his deed. The elements of the criminal-brought-to-justice formula are the following: youth, upbringing, or past deeds of
criminal; crucial crime and events leading to it; pursuit, capture, and trial; execution.

The crime described in the murdered-girl formula is a particularly shocking one—trust betrayed by one whom, above all
others, one should be able to trust. In the criminal-brought-to-
justice formula, the particular crime committed is not very important. It is merely alluded to or given cursory treatment. The
central episode, the one requiring the greatest number of verses,
is the fall of the criminal—his incarceration, his family's grief,
his execution. While the criminal ballad concentrates on the
punishment, the murdered-girl ballad concentrates on the
crime.

Sometimes the murdered-girl formula combines with the second half of the criminal formula to produce ballads in which
the capture and punishment of the lover-murderer are reported.
Pearl Bryan V is an example among the Pearl Bryan ballads.
Other murdered-girl ballads of this type are "Rose Connoley"
(Laws F 6), "The Wexford Girl" (Laws P 35), and early forms
of "Omie Wise" (Laws F 4). The fact that this combination
occurs repeatedly may lead to the conclusion that it constitutes
a separate formula. There is a strong tendency for this combination to break down, however, and for the criminal half of the
formula to disappear. Chapter 3 documents this process in the
case of the Pearl Bryan ballads. The histories of "Pretty Polly"
(Laws P 36) and "Omie Wise," two common murdered-girl
ballads, show the power of the murdered-girl formula to cast
out extraneous matter. Early texts of these ballads relate the
punishment of the murderer, while later texts end with the

crime itself.[1] If Phillips Barry is right in saying that "The Jealous Lover" derives in part from a British broadside, "The Murder of Betsy Smith," then the enormously popular "Jealous
Lover" is another case in point.[2] "The Murder of Betsy Smith"
recounts the murderer's capture and removal to prison where
"in rattling chains he is confined," while "The Jealous Lover"
normally ends with the abandonment of the girl's body.

The newspapers tended to break down the events they related into two stories, one with Pearl Bryan at its center and one
with Scott Jackson at its center. The Pearl Bryan–oriented story
followed the murdered-girl formula, while the Scott Jackson
story was influenced by the criminal-brought-to-justice formula. When describing events up to the point when Pearl was
murdered, the newspapers related events in terms of her trust
in Jackson, her innocence, her attachment to family, his betrayal of her, the cab ride to a lonely spot in the Kentucky Highlands,[3] her helplessness to save herself, and the abandoning of
her body. When the newspapers turned their attention to Jackson, they told his story in criminal-brought-to-justice terms, re-
counting his checkered past and concentrating on events in
court, in jail, and on the scaffold.

The newspapers did, of course, present many more items
than those falling into the above categories. The function of a

[1] The early texts of "Pretty Polly" punish the lover-murderer by super-
natural means. "Omie Wise," more conventionally, relies on the mills of
justice; but, although the criminal is captured and tried, he is not convicted. This violation of formula is due to the fact that "Omie Wise" at this
point in time had not yet liberated itself from the facts of a real murder
case on which the song was based; in fact, the accused murderer could
not be convicted.

[2] Phillips Barry, "Fair Florella," *American Speech* 3 (1928): 441.

[3] Although the spot where the body was found was near a road in a
fairly heavily populated small-farm area surrounding a fort, the newspapers habitually referred to the spot as a "secluded place" near a "lonely
road," or as being in the "bleak hills of the Kentucky Highlands."

newspaper is, presumably, to record what does happen even when it doesn't follow a formula. But there was a tendency to interpret events in terms of formula, even when distortion was required to accomplish it. This tension between fact and formula in newspaper accounts is documented in Chapter 2. Perhaps the outstanding example of this tension is the difficulty that both newspapers and ballads had in accounting for Walling's involvement in the murder. In the murdered-girl formula the murderer of the girl is her lover. Ballads and newspapers were faced with the problem of accommodating to this formula the fact that two men were convicted and executed for the crime. In the ballads the tendency is to forget Walling or to make of him a subsidiary figure. This device is documented in Chapter 3. The approach taken by the papers was to assign to Walling the role of Jackson's tool or puppet. Although four hands may have assisted at Pearl Bryan's demise, only one will was at work. The story of Pearl Bryan's fate thus becomes an encounter between but two personalities or two interests—the trusting girl and the lover-murderer.

In Chapter 2 another example of the influence of the murdered-girl formula was seen in the increasing tendency, in time, for the ballads to suppress the fact that Pearl was beheaded. In other murdered-girl ballads victims are stabbed, beaten, drowned, and poisoned, but beheading is not in the repertoire of allowable methods. Thus, a sensational feature of a story, which one might expect to be memorable and hence retained, is quick to disappear.

Ballad accounts and newspaper accounts of the Pearl Bryan story shared a stereotyped cast of characters. The murdered girl is innocent, trusting, and helpless vis-à-vis the lover-murderer. She has a family to grieve after her. The lover-murderer is clever and brutal. In the ballads, the lover-murderer rarely has a family to grieve after him, for the sorrowing family of the condemned man belongs to the criminal-brought-to-justice formula. The sorrowing families or aged parents may occur in either plot formula, but in the murdered-girl formula they belong to the girl, and in the criminal-brought-to-justice formula they belong to the criminal.[4]

The newspapers cast Scott Jackson in two roles, that of lover-murderer and that of a criminal brought to justice. The ballads usually saw him as lover-murderer only and tended to lose any criminal-brought-to-justice verses. In the newspapers, on the other hand, we have endless visit-in-jail scenes, weeping families, last-day scenes, and scaffold scenes. The Pearl Bryan ballads have no such scenes revolving around Jackson. The criminal elements found in Pearl Bryan ballads consist of pursuit and trial and pleading parent. In the pleading-parent scene, however, it is Mrs. Walling rather than Mrs. Jackson who addresses the jury.[5] Since Jackson is the central figure and principal murderer, one might expect the ballads to represent his mother pleading to the bar and tearing her old gray locks. But ballad murderers of their sweethearts do not have aged parents pleading for them in court. I suspect that this is because weeping-relative and pleading-parent scenes express a certain amount of sympathy for the prisoner, a sentiment usually denied the lover-murderer. Walling's crime, on the other hand, is not murdering his sweetheart but assisting at *a* murder. The crim-

---

[4] It is not claimed, of course, that these attributes characterize every ballad about a murdered sweetheart or captured criminal, but that this is the pattern which most follow or toward which they develop. It is common enough to be considered a real characteristic of American balladry.

[5] There is one exception. Ellie Sibert, on a Library of Congress recording made in 1937, has Jackson's mother do the pleading. However, she pauses before naming her, as though uncertain what name to put in. Walling is barely mentioned in this text; since he appears to be on his way out in this version of the ballad, the pleading-parent elements that remain have been attached, with hesitation, to Jackson.

inal of the criminal-brought-to-justice formula may commit murder, but seldom one so loathsome as killing his trusting sweetheart.[6] For this reason, I think it would be a strain on the formula for Scott Jackson's mother to plead for her son, but not for Walling's mother to do so.

In very general terms, the murdered-girl formula may be seen as a sequence of trust followed by betrayal. If the criminal-brought-to-justice pattern is tacked on at the end, the trust-betrayal sequence adds a third element, retribution. Retribution, however, tends to disappear in ballads about the lover-murderer, whose crime is particularly odious, while it is central in ballads about the criminal, whose crime is more forgivable.

There is a repeated type of narrative device found in both ballad and newspaper accounts, a dramatic encounter that heightens the emotional impact of a scene. This device is the plea followed by refusal. Pearl Bryan's sister, on her knees, begging for her sister's head, was presented in vivid detail to newspaper readers over and over again.[7] Chapter 2 describes newspaper treatment of Mrs. Walling's plea to the Bryan family: even though no reporter was present, the scene was presented pictorially and dramatically. Mrs. Walling's plea to Jackson to confess and exonerate Walling was also given many column inches, as were the pleas made by both the prisoners and their families for executive clemency. The plea-refusal mini-drama was a standard feature of the Pearl Bryan story as it was presented in newspapers.

All the Pearl Bryan ballads include the plea-refusal sequence. Pearl pleads for her life, but Jackson will not be swayed. Wall-

[6] The only exception I know is "Bad Companions" (Laws E 15).

[7] As pointed out in Chapter 2, Pearl's sister did not in fact go down on her knees to plead for Pearl's head. The kneeling position crept into the story later and became standard for the scene. Kneeling position is, of course, customary in ballads when a plea is to be made.

ing's mother pleads for Walling's life, but the jury condemns him anyway. Pearl's sister pleads with Jackson for Pearl's head, but Jackson answers coldly. Less often, Pearl pleads with Jackson to make a respectable woman of her, but he refuses. In one unusual verse, six young ladies plead for bail for the criminals, but they are refused.[8] Pleas refused are a common feature of both murdered-girl and criminal-brought-to-justice ballads. It is a rare murdered-girl ballad that omits a scene in which the girl pleads for her life, and it is a rare criminal-brought-to-justice ballad in which neither the criminal nor his parents or friends appeal to the law for his life or liberty.

It may at first appear that in ballads centering on pathos, such as murdered-girl or criminal ballads, the granting of a plea would spoil the pathos or hinder the story line. This is not necessarily true. A popular nineteenth-century ballad, "The Lightning Express,"[9] bases its pathos on the capitulation of a train conductor and passengers to a little boy's plea. "East-bound Train"[10] tells a similar story about a little girl. In "The Prisoner at the Bar,"[11] the plea of a sweetheart to the law is successful.

A common pattern in Anglo-American balladry is a series of refusals followed by capitulation, for example, "Hangman"

[8] This verse may be inspired by a memory of the fact that many young women were fascinated by Jackson and Walling: they appeared in droves at the trials; they visited both in prison; they sent presents to the prisoners; they wrote them letters; several claimed to be the real sweethearts of one or the other of the men; and two young women on their own initiative sacrificed their reputations in vain attempts to provide alibis for the men. The psychosocial implications of such behavior are intriguing but beyond the scope of this study.

[9] Original title "Please Mister Conductor"; words and music by J. F. Helf and E. P. Moran; published by Hawley, Haviland, & Co., 1898. This song has been recovered frequently from oral tradition.

[10] Original title "Going for a Pardon"; words by J. Thornton and C. Hauenschild, music by J. Thornton; published by Jos. Stern & Co., 1896. Like the above, this ballad appears in oral tradition.

[11] Vance Randolph, *Ozark Folksongs*, IV, 348.

(Child 95), "The False Lover Won Back" (Child 218), and "The Cruel War" (Laws O 33). Other stories advanced by pleas granted include "The Maid on the Shore" (Laws K 27), "The Three Butchers" (Laws L 4), and "Henry Green" (Laws F 14). Given all the possibilities that are actually used, it seems clear that the refusal of a plea is not required to advance a story line, even a tragic one. A number of additional possibilities that are not used may be considered: the murdered girl makes a dying request that is granted; she is allowed to select the form of her demise or is allowed some other boon (as in the case of Child 4, "Lady Isabel and the Elf Knight"); the murderer tells the pleading parent that the head is in some inaccessible spot or that he destroyed it; the law capitulates to the aged parent's request, but the pardon comes too late.

One formulaic representation found frequently in newspaper accounts but rarely in ballads is the city-country opposition. The newspapers represented the city as the source of sophistication and evil, while the country offered simplicity and innocence.[12] Consider the following newspaper passages:

Lured from Her Peace-
ful Country Home

——

To Her Death in the Dark
Mazes of a Great
City—The Crime
of the Century[13]

[12] This opposition of urban and rural values is found in lyric folksongs, interestingly enough. It is often found in topical songs and in nineteenth-century pop songs that have become traditional. The theme is a common one in modern country-western songs. See Norm Cohen, "Urban vs. Rural Values in Country and Pop Songs: A Review Essay," *JEMF Quarterly* 6 (Summer 1970): 62–64.

[13] *Enquirer* (Cincinnati), March 21, 1897. More of this passage is given in Chapter 2.

"I cannot give a very good description of the young woman. I saw the left side of her face. The wind was blowing the cape about her. She was clutching at her hat, which had feathers on it. She was plump, and her fresh, clean appearance showed she was from the country."[14]

It will be remembered that when Pearl's body was first found she was described as "an abandoned woman from Cincinnati" and "a woman of the town." As soon as it was discovered that the corpse was pregnant the description changed to "innocent trusting girl whose only offense was having loved too well." One of the attending doctors at the post-mortem apparently decided that if she was innocent and trusting she must be from the country, for he said, "The girl, in my opinion, was from the country and was comparatively innocent."[15]

Scott Jackson was contrasted with the simple country girl: "Pearl Bryan, the country girl, had met her horrid death in Cincinnati. Her headless body was lying unidentified in the muck at Newport . . . and Scott Jackson, dental student, was walking the streets of Cincinnati free and as yet unsuspected."[16] Jackson's worldly experiences in big cities were stressed: "His first business experience was that of messenger boy for the Pennsylvania Company at Jersey City, where he worked three years, being finally discharged for complicity in an embezzlement. . . . Then he drifted to New York City, where he worked in a gent's furnishing store for about a year, and later acted as city drummer for a similar house."[17] Jackson's knowledge and education, his association with "intellectuals," such as his friend the physician, are shown:

14 *Daily Banner Times* (Greencastle), May 1, 1896.

15 *Enquirer* (Cincinnati), February 4, 1896. More of this quotation appears in Chapter 2.

16 Ibid., April 25, 1896.

17 *Evening Post* (Louisville), March 20, 1897.

Jackson was determined to be rid of the trusting country girl he ruined. For days before Pearl Bryan's arrival in the city he had been reading up books on poisons, hunting for a poison that would kill quickly.

He evidently gave up the idea of using the acid, which the physician friend had suggested, and decided upon cocaine. Taking twenty grains of the dangerous drug, he dissolved it in eighty grains of water, making what is known as a 25 per cent solution, and an extraordinarily strong one. A 4 per cent solution is the one used for ordinary medical purposes.[18]

In the early summer of 1895 all the girls in Greencastle were talking about an event which was soon to happen. Scott Jackson was coming home. He had been away for some time, and those who had known him remembered him as a handsome young fellow. His career had been checkered just enough to give him that indefinable something which is fascinating to a young girl. Besides that he was bright and smart, and came of a good family, and a brilliant future had been predicted for him. . . . It was in the afternoon when he jumped from a westbound train, and, valise in hand, marched through the quiet, country town to the unpretentious one-story brick where his mother lived—the home of his childhood days.[19]

In other accounts his knowledge of saloons and entertainment houses in Cincinnati, his experiences with women, and his knowledge of the latest tunes and latest styles were described. Altogether Jackson was shown as clever, resourceful, and well educated, a small-town boy who followed his ambition to the big city and became a dental student in the metropolis of his area, Cincinnati. He was attracted to the vice and corruption of the big city and was soon familiar with it all. When he discovered Pearl's condition, it was to Cincinnati that he urged her

[18] Ibid., February 8, 1896.
[19] *Enquirer* (Cincinnati), April 19, 1896.

to come, where he would take care of her. In contrast to this was placed the "quiet country town," "the home of his boyhood days," where he met the innocent maiden whom he brought to the city to destroy.

In the ballads, this country-city opposition does not appear, except perhaps by implication. Pearl Bryan I tells us that Pearl was murdered just outside of Cincinnati, "far away from friends and home." It might be inferred that, if Pearl did not come from Cincinnati, she came from the surrounding countryside. Pearl Bryan V says:

> Pearl went to Cincinnata
> She had not been there before
> Led astray by Scott Jackson
> To never see Mama no more

This verse implies that Pearl was led astray after she came to Cincinnati and thus associates vice and the city. Her simple background may be indicated in the line "She had not been there before." Pearl Bryans I and V both say that the fatal ride was taken in a cab, suggesting an urban area. All in all, there is little to indicate any sense of country-city contrast in the ballads. The lack of this contrast suggests that ballad makers ignored a formula presented to them by the newspapers from which they drew their information. Why, when they accepted formulae of plot, character, scene, and epithet provided by newspapers, did they reject this one? I think it is because the murdered-girl formula does not include it. The criminal-brought-to-justice formula does sometimes describe the criminal's life of dissipation in the city:

> I am a reckless ramblin' boy
> To many an' many I wish you joy
> To Columbus City I made my way

To spend my money at the balls an' plays[20]

I bid adieu to loved ones
To home I said farewell
And I landed in Chicago
In the very depths of hell[21]

The newspapers offered to ballad makers ready-made material for two different types of ballads, the murdered-girl type and the criminal-brought-to-justice type. Given the nature of the crime, the ballad muse could choose only the murdered-girl formula. While newspapers might be able to present a criminal-brought-to-justice story in which the crime was the murder of a trusting sweetheart, such an attempt could scarcely succeed in a ballad, as has been documented in the case of Pearl Bryan V. If Scott Jackson's crime had been, for example, the murder of a rival in love, all other elements of the tragedy could have been unchanged and there still would have been no lonely walk and no plea for life in the ballads. The ballads would have begun, "My name it is Scott Jackson," and would have proceeded along conventional criminal lines. It would have been Scott Jackson's mother, not Walling's, who appeared to plead for his life, and the ballads would have spent the majority of their verses on the visits of weeping relatives to the prison and on Jackson's farewell at the gallows.

[20] Vance Randolph, *Ozark Folksongs*, "The Rambling Boy," A Text, II, 84.

[21] Ibid., "Bad Companions," B Text, II, 140.

APPENDIX

The following pages list all the Pearl Bryan ballads known to me, excluding commercial recordings made recently by non-traditional singers of the "folksong revival." The texts are arranged by types as they have been outlined in this study, and within each type by date of collection. Where the informant has given a date earlier than the date of collection as the date the song was learned, I have listed the song under the date learned, but I have indicated in parentheses the caution "dated by informant." While an informant's memory may not be entirely accurate in all cases, songs are listed under dates given by informants in order to indicate the earliest date a song can be in tradition. In some cases, where the collector has given no date for a text, I have dated texts simply as "pre-1958," for instance, where 1958 is the date of publication of the collection. In some cases, although no date is given for a particular song, an introduction to the collection as a whole or some other source will give a date or approximate date at which the entire collection was made; in these cases there is a question mark after the date listing, indicating that the date given is a probability though not a certainty of the date of collection.

The data on each song are listed as follows: After the date of collection or of learning the song, the source for the text is given according to the abbreviation schedule shown below. The source is followed by the informant's name and location. If date and location are given for the contributor of the text rather than for the informant, as in Paul Brewster's *Ballads and Songs of Indiana*, this information is given with the contributor's name. The number of stanzas is given next, a stanza being counted as a completed rhyme scheme. Most stanzas, as listed here, consist of the following type of short quatrain:

> Deep, deep in a lonely valley
> Where the violets fade and bloom
> There sleeps my own Pearl Bryan
> So silent in the tomb

Each text is given in terms of the classification scheme developed in this study and is listed, for instance, as so many stanzas of Pearl Bryan II, followed by so many stanzas of Pearl Bryan I. Thus, the notation "12v. PB II, 1v. PB I" indicates that the text consists of twelve stanzas of Pearl Bryan II followed by one stanza of Pearl Bryan I. If the text has a chorus, it is so noted. Also indicated in parentheses is the appearance, when it occurs, of the "album" verse associated with Pearl Bryans II and V, discussed in Chapter 2.

ABBREVIATIONS USED

ACC: Author's collection.

ACWF: Archive of California and Western Folklore, University of California, Los Angeles.

Brewster, *BSI*: Paul Brewster, *Ballads and Songs of Indiana*, pp. 283–289.

Brown, *NCF*: Frank C. Brown, *The Frank C. Brown Collection of North Carolina Folklore*, II, 588.

Burt, *AMB*: Olive W. Burt, *American Murder Ballads and Their Stories*, pp. 31–32.

Burton, *ETC*: Thomas G. Burton and Ambrose N. Manning, *The East Tennessee State University Collection of Folklore: Folksongs*, p. 77.

Cambiaire, *ETWV*: Celestin Pierre Cambiaire, *East Tennessee and Western Virginia Mountain Ballads*, p. 109.

Combs, *FSSUS*: Josiah Combs, *Folk-Songs of the Southern United States*, p. 174.

Cox, *FSS*: John Harrington Cox, *Folk-Songs of the South*, pp. 197–202.

Eddy, *BSO*: Mary O. Eddy, *Ballads and Songs from Ohio*, pp. 241–243.

Finger, *FB*: Charles J. Finger, *Frontier Ballads*, pp. 80–81.

Gordon MSS: Robert W. Gordon, unpublished mss. at the Library of Congress, Washington, D.C.

Hamilton MSS: Emory L. Hamilton, "Folk Songs of the Cumberlands," collected for Federal Writers' Project, WPA, 1939–1940. Unpublished mss. at Clinch Valley College, Wise, Va. A copy of the mss. is in the Archive of American Folk Song, Library of Congress, Washington, D.C.

Henry, *FSSH*: M. E. Henry, *Folk-Songs from the Southern Highlands*, pp. 209, 212.

Henry, "Notes 1929": M. E. Henry, "Notes and Queries," *Journal of American Folklore* 42 (1929): 301–303.

Henry, "Notes 1943": M. E. Henry, "Notes and Queries," *Journal of American Folklore* 56 (1943): 139–140.

Henry, "Still More": M. E. Henry, "Still More Ballads and Folk-Songs from the Southern Highlands," *Journal of American Folklore* 45 (1932): 132–134.

Huff MSS: Unpublished mss., a group of hand-written songs from members of the Huff family, 1932–1934, Leslie Co., Ky.; at the Library of Congress, Archive of Folk Song, Washington, D.C.

LC Rec: Library of Congress Recordings, Archive of Folk Song, Library of Congress, Washington, D.C.

Morris, *FF*: A. C. Morris, *Folksongs of Florida*, p. 79.

Musick, "West Va.": Ruth Ann Musick, "West Virginia Songs of Murder," *West Virginia Folklore* 7, no. 4 (1957): 63.

Neely & Spargo, *TSSI*: Charles Neely and J. W. Spargo, *Tales and Songs of Southern Illinois*, pp. 157–160.

Perrow, "Songs": E. C. Perrow, "Songs and Rhymes from the South," *Journal of American Folklore* 28 (1915): 168.

Randolph, *OF*: Vance Randolph, *Ozark Folksongs*, II, 48.

Scarborough MSS: Dorothy Scarborough, unpublished mss. at Baylor University, Waco, Texas. [Copy of text from the mss. furnished by Marina Bokelman.]

Sharp MSS: Cecil Sharp, unpublished mss. copy, Houghton Library, Harvard University, Cambridge, Mass. [Copies of texts from the mss. furnished by D. K. Wilgus, University of California, Los Angeles.]

WKFA (WKU): Western Kentucky Folklore Archive, University of California, Los Angeles, California. [Copies of materials at *WKFA* are also on deposit at Western Kentucky University, Bowling Green, Kentucky.]

Williams, *BS*: Cratis Williams, "Ballads and Songs," p. 130.

Wilson, "Pearl": Ann Scott Wilson, "Pearl Bryan," *Southern Folklore Quarterly* 3 (1939): 15–19.

THE TEXTS

Pearl Bryan I

A. *Dalhart Group*

1926.   Dalhart, Vernon, "Pearl Bryan." Vocalion Master E 3902 (recorded Oct. 5, 1926). Vocalion 5015 (under pseud. Jep Fuller; released ca. Feb. 1927). 12v. Dalhart PB I.

1926.   Dalhart, Vernon, "Pearl Bryan." Columbia Master W 142896 (recorded Nov. 1, 1926). Columbia 15169-D (under pseud. Al Craver; released Aug. 30, 1927). 12v. Dalhart PB I.

1927.   Dalhart, Vernon, "Pearl Bryan." Okeh Master W-80-373-B (recorded Feb. 1, 1927, in NY). Okeh 45090 (under pseud. Tobe Little; released Mar. 25, 1927). 12v. Dalhart PB I.

1930?   M. M. Cole Publishing Co., Chicago, published a number of songbooks with different titles, using the same plates for the songs. The following songbooks use the same plate for "Pearl Bryan," which consists of 12v. Dalhart PB I:

    1. "Carson J. Robison's World's Greatest Collection of Mountain Ballads and Old Time Songs" (1930).

    2. "KFBI Songs of the Plains."

    3. "Play and Sing. America's Greatest Collection of Old Time Songs and Mountain Ballads."

    4. "Tiny Texan World's Greatest Collection of Cowboy and Mountain Ballads" (1930).

pre-1934.   Huff MSS: Anon., n.d. 12v. Dalhart PB I.

1935.   Brewster, *BSI*: Mrs. Jesse N. Engler, Pike Co. Contrib. by Mrs. Dora McAtee, Oakland City, Gibson Co., 1935. 6v. Dalhart PB I.

1937.   Williams, *BS*: Mrs. Mabel Barber, Caines Creek, Lawrence Co., Ky., n.d. 12v. Dalhart PB I.

1940.   Hamilton MSS: Mrs. Myrtle Horton, Scott Co., Va. 12v. Dalhart PB I.

1957.   *WKFA*: Gladys Pace, Nobob, Barren Co. Tape T-7-14. 12v. Dalhart PB I.

1959.   *WKFA*: Mrs. Allen Driscoll, Jefferson Co. 12v. Dalhart PB I.

1967.   *ACC*: Miss Marion Enerson, Dennison, Minn. Text copied from book she called "Mountain Songs." It is identical to text found in series put out by M. M. Cole Publishing Co., mentioned above under year 1930. 12v. Dalhart PB I.

B. *Non-Dalhart Group*

1927.   Gordon MSS: B. M. Carpenter, Sulphur, Ky. 8v. & chorus, PB I.

1927.   Gordon MSS: Mrs. G. O. Collins, Clyde, Tex. 11v. & 2v. chorus, PB I.

1927?   Gordon MSS: Bertha Zoller(?), Billings, Mo. 12v. & chorus, PB I.

1935.   Brewster, *BSI*: Miss Edith Del Hopkins, Boonville, Warrick Co. 1v. PB I.

1949.   *WKFA*: Mrs. Clay Reid, Symsonia, Graves Co. 9v. & chorus, PB I.

1950.   *WKFA*: Mrs. Lewis Good, Hopkins Co. 8v. PB I.

1953.   *WKFA*: Mrs. Martha Hunsucker, Seymour, Ind. [texts sent her "by four people in Kentucky"]. Published in the *Courier-Journal* (Louisville), "Greetings" column, edited by Allan M. Trout, on June 10, 1953. 6v. PB I.

1956.   *WKFA*: Mrs. Hubert Hallmark, Curdsville, Daviess Co. Tape T-7-1. 6v. PB I.

pre-1958.   Burt, *AMB*: Miss Eleanor Buchanan, contributor. 8v. PB I.

1961?   *WKFA*: Pearl Herrin, Providence. 5v. PB I.

1966.   *ACC*: Miss Clara Nussbaumer, West Unity, Ohio. 12v. & chorus, PB I.

C. *Dalhart–Non-Dalhart Mixtures*

1969.   *Renfro Valley Bugle*, Renfro Valley, Ky., July 1969. 2v. PB I, 10v. Dalhart PB I.

D. *Mixed Texts of Pearl Bryan I*

1931.   Gordon MSS: Miss Eula Adkins, Whitley Co., Ky. In Mary Newcomb mss. ½v. PB V, 1½v. PB I.

1935.   Brewster, *BSI*: Mrs. Flossie Blythe. Contrib. by Miss Larue
         Smith and Miss Frances Hunt, Oakland City, Gibson Co. 8v.
         PB I, 5v. PB V.
1948.   *WKFA*: Mrs. W. E. Clark, Mayfield. 4v. PB II, 1v. PB I or
         VI.
1964?   *The Phipps Family*, Folkways Records FA 2375. 6v. Dalhart
         PB I, 1v. unidentified, 2v. PB II, 2v. unidentified.
1966.   *ACC*: J. O. Ward, Scottsburg, Ind. 1v. PB I, 6v. PB II.
1966.   Burton, *ETC*: Mrs. Mary Coyle [learned from print]. 4v.
         PB I, 2v. PB V, 2v. PB I.
1967.   Rev. Dallas Turner (under pseud. "Nevada Slim"), "Pearl
         Bryon," Rural Rhythm RRNS 166-A. Recomposition from
         PB I, II, V.

Pearl Bryan II

pre-1900.   (Dated by informant). Collected 1954. *WKFA*: Mrs.
             John Marquess, Trigg Co. 6v. PB II.
1903–1905.   (Dated by informant). Collected 1925. Gordon MSS:
             Earl Morgan, St. Petersburg, Fla. 2v. PB II.
1910.   (Dated by informant). Collected 1925? Gordon MSS: Mrs.
             F. W. Billings, Dalton, Mass. 8v. PB II, 1v. unidentified.
1912.   (Dated by informant). Collected 1915. Cox, *FSS*: Miss
             Marion Rennar. Contrib. by Miss Nellie Donley, Morgan-
             town, Monongalia Co., W.Va. 9v. PB II.
1913.   Burt, *AMB*: Anon., Morgan Co., Utah. 1v. PB II.
1913.   Perrow, "Songs": E. N. Caldwell, N.C. 12v. PB II.
1916.   Cox, *FSS*: Prof. Walter Barnes, Fairmont, Marion Co., W.Va.
             9v. PB II.
1916.   Cox, *FSS*: Miss Janet Cook. Contrib. by Prof. Walter Barnes,
             Fairmont, Marion Co., W.Va. 1v. PB II.
1916.   (Dated by informant). Collected 1938. LC Rec: Sgt. A.
             Kirkheart, Fort Thomas, Ky. [Reports he learned song in
             W.Va.] AAFS 1699A. 8½v. PB II.
1919.   *ACC*: Delphia Shroyer, Ralston, Okla. Contrib. by Mrs.
             Nora M. Ryers, Coolidge, Ariz., 1967. 9v. PB II.
1923.   Brown, *NCF*: Miss Zilpah Frisbie, Marion, McDowell Co.
             7v. PB II.
1924.   Combs, *FSSUS*: Lona Woofter, Glenville, Gilmer Co.,
             W.Va. 8v. & chorus, PB II.

1925. (Dated by informant). Collected 1959. *WKFA*: Mrs. Vera Reagan Martin, ballet collection; Tompkinsville, Monroe Co. Tape T-7-33. 11v. PB II.

1926. Burnett, Richard, and Leonard Rutherford, "Pearl Bryan." Columbia Master W 143097 (recorded Nov. 6, 1926, Atlanta). Columbia 15113-D (as Burnett and Rutherford; released Jan. 10, 1927). Reissued on County 522. 9v. PB II (includes "album" verse).

pre-1927. Finger, *FB*: Anon. 1v. PB II.

1927. Harvey, Roy, and Bob Hoke (plus unidentified banjo player, probably C. Poole), "Pearl Bryant." Gennett Master GEX-887 (recorded Sept. 26, 1927, NY). Supertone 9246 (under pseud. "The Three Kentucky Serenaders," released spring, 1929). Silvertone 5181 (under pseud. "The Three Kentucky Serenaders," released mid-1928 or earlier). Silvertone 8147 (under pseud. "The Three Kentucky Serenaders," released fall, 1928). All consist of 10v. PB II.

1927. Gordon MSS: Miss Virginia Berkley, Point Pleasant, W.Va. 8v. & chorus, PB II.

1927. Gordon MSS: Gertrude M. Brooks, Winchester, Ky. 12v. PB II.

1927. Gordon MSS: Mrs. G. O. Collins, Clyde, Texas. Sent her from Rita Langford, Coxs Mills, W.Va. 12v. PB II.

1927. Gordon MSS: Miss Myrtle Delaney, Everett, Wash. Contrib. by Olive C. Kay. 9v. PB II.

1927. Gordon MSS: Mildred Freeman, Moatsville, W.Va. 8½v. PB II.

1927. Gordon MSS: Olive C. Kay, Evans, W.Va. 8v. PB II, 1v. unidentified.

1927. Gordon MSS: Laura M. Klinefelter, Steele, N.Dak. 12v. PB II.

1927. Gordon MSS: Frances Ollender, Alton, W.Va. 13v. PB II.

1927. Gordon MSS: Mae Slaubaugh, Horse Shoe Run, W.Va. 9v. PB II.

1927. Gordon MSS: Tina Storms, Stillwater, Okla. 12v. PB II.

1927? Gordon MSS: Anon. 8v. PB II, 1v. unidentified.

1927? Gordon MSS: Gladys K. Fletcher. 10v. PB II.

1927? Gordon MSS: Miss Eunice Hall, Marietta, Ohio. 5v. PB II.

1927? Gordon MSS: Rita Langford, Coxs Mills, W.Va. Contrib. by both Mrs. G. O. Collins, Clyde, Texas, and Olive C. Kay, Evans, W.Va. 12v. PB II.

1927? Gordon MSS: Mary Newcomb mss., "additional." 11v. PB II.

1927? Gordon MSS: Bertha Zoller, Billings, Mo. 9v. PB II.

1928. (Dated by informant). Collected 1936. Wilson, "Pearl": Trula Lawson, Morgantown, W.Va. 6v. PB II.

1928. Randolph, *OF*: Mrs. Coral Almy Wilson, Zinc, Ark. 8v. PB II (includes "album" verse).

1928. Bradley Kincaid. "My Favorite Mountain Ballads and Old-Time Songs," p. 17.

1929. Bradley Kincaid. "Pearl Bryan." Gennett Master 14743 (recorded Jan. 28, 1929, Richmond, Ind.). Champion 15731 (under pseud. "Dan Hughey," released June 1, 1929). Supertone 9404 (released fall, 1929). Gennett 6823 (released June 1929). All consist of 12v. PB II.

1933–1937. Morris, *FF*: Miss Evelyn Braddock, Sanderson. 8v. PB II.

pre-1934. Cambiaire, *ETWV*: Edison Brown, E. Tenn. 5v. PB II.

1935. Brewster, *BSI*: Mrs. Hiram Vaughan. Contrib. by Miss Sylvia Vaughan, Oakland City, Gibson Co. 12v. PB II.

1935–1937. Neely & Spargo, *TSSI*: Anon., Egypt. 14v. PB II.

1938. (Dated by informant). Collected 1955. *WKFA*: T. P. Sholar, Trigg Co. 9v. PB II.

1938. LC Rec: Thelma, Beatrice, and Irene Scruggs, Burnsville, Miss. AAFS 1706 B 2. 6v. PB II.

1939. LC Rec: Mrs. Lola Canoy, Magee, Miss. AAFS 3058 B 1. 7v. PB II.

1940. LC Rec: Lois Judd, Arvin, Calif. AAFS 4102 B. 10v. PB II.

1948. *WKFA*: Mrs. Jewel Cardwell, Hickman, Fulton Co. 6v. PB II.

1949. *WKFA*: Mr. Walter Miles, ballet, Elva, Marshall Co. 9v. PB II.

1953. *WFKA*: Mrs. G. H. Basham, Rogers Springs, Grayson Co. 5v. PB II.

1953. *WKFA*: Mrs. T. H. Hughes, Russellville, Mrs. J. A. Jones, Glasgow, and Mrs. Reia Clark, Little Barren, Ky. Published in the *Courier-Journal* (Louisville), "Greetings" column, edited by Allan M. Trout, on June 9, 1953. 10v. PB II.

1955. *WKFA*: Mrs. Mint Noel, Trigg Co. 13v. PB II.

1955. *WKFA*: Bonne Thomas. 1v. PB II.
1956. *WKFA*: Mary Bridges, Bowling Green, Warren Co. 7v. PB II.
1956. *WKFA*: Flossie Huddlestone, Burkesville. 5v. PB II (includes "album" verse).
1957. *WKFA*: Gladys Pace, Nobob, Barren Co. Tape T-7-14. 8v. PB II.
1958. *WKFA*: Wayne Elmore, Barnes Co. 9½v. PB II.
1958. *WKFA*: Bertha Kingrey, Scottsville. 7v. PB II.
1958. *WKFA*: *Daily News* (Park City), May 20, 1958, letter to the editor from Fletcher Cochrane, Park City. 4v. PB II.
1959. *WKFA*: Mrs. Hubert Cherry, ballet, Bowling Green, Warren Co. 4v. PB II.
1959. *WKFA*: Wilma Pace Grace, Temple Hill, Barren Co. 8v. PB II.
1959. *WKFA*: Mrs. Meyer Smith, Breckinridge Co. 9v. PB II.
1960. *WKFA*: Fielding Fentress, Kingswood. 1v. PB II.
1961. *WKFA*: Mrs. Leon Curtis, Glasgow. Tape T-7-86. 5v. PB II.
1961. *WKFA*: Mrs. May Rhoton, Tompkinsville, Monroe Co. 8v. PB II, 1v. unidentified.
1962. *WKFA*: Lorene Burden, Louisville. 3v. PB II.
1962. *WKFA*: Mrs. Darrell Pace, Summer Shade. 8v. PB II.
1962. *WKFA*: Jeannie Chancellor Freeman, ballet book, Mayfield. 13v. PB II.
1962. *WKFA*: Mrs. Floy C. Lyons, Cloverport, Breckinridge Co. Tape T-7-123. 13v. PB II.
1963. *WKFA*: Mrs. Artha White, Albany. ½v. PB II.
1964. *WKFA*: Anon., Russell Springs. 7v. PB II (includes "album" verse).
1964. *WKFA*: Mrs. Nettie Jarboe, Hancock Co. 2v. PB II.
1965. *WKFA*: *Courier-Journal* (Louisville), "Greetings" column, edited by Allan M. Trout, April 3, 1965. Letter from Mrs. S. J. Oliver, Glasgow. 10v. PB II.
1966. *ACC*: Mrs. Martha Quick, Linn, Mo. 12v. PB II.
1967. *ACWF*: Mrs. Garland Sanburg, McComb, Miss. Contrib. by J. W. Bond, Los Angeles. 10v. PB II.
pre-1968. *WKFA*: Mrs. Ella B. Bruce, Breckinridge Co. 8½v. PB II.
1968. *ACC*: Herbert Shellans, Phoenix, Ariz. 7v. PB II.

Mixed Texts of Pearl Bryan II

1948. *WKFA*: Mrs. W. E. Clark, Mayfield. 4v. PB II, 1v. PB I
       or V.
1966. *ACC*: J. O. Ward, Scottsburg, Ind. 1v. PB I, 6v. PB II.

Pearl Bryan III

1925. Henry, *FSSH*: Granville Gadsey, Breathitt Co., Ky. 8v. PB
       III. [Same text given also in Henry, "Notes 1929."]
1927. Gordon MSS: Olive C. Kay, Evans, W.Va. 7v. PB III.
1931. Gordon MSS: Miss Audrey Cline, Rinard Mills, Ohio, n.d.
       In Mary Newcomb mss., 1931. 8v. PB III.
1937. LC Rec: R. C. Macfarland, Salyersville, Ky. AAFS 1567 B
       1. 2v. PB III.
pre-1939. Eddy, *BSO*: Mrs. Rozetta Lozier, Perrysville. 6v. PB III.
1953. *WKFA*: *Courier-Journal* (Louisville), "Greetings" column,
       edited by Allan M. Trout, June 16, 1953. Letter from Thom-
       as F. Stone, Campbellsville. 8v. PB III.

Pearl Bryan IV

1927. Gordon MSS: Millicent Lawler, Mazomaine, Wisc. 10v. &
       chorus, PB IV.
pre-1939. Eddy, *BSO*: Mrs. Rozetta Lozier, Perrysville. 6v. PB IV.

Mixed Texts of Pearl Bryan IV

1958. Forrest Lewis, Parksville, Ky. From unpublished field re-
       cording made by Ed Kahn of Los Angeles, Calif. 1v. PB IV,
       2v. "The Band Played On," 2v. PB VI, 1v. unidentified, 2v.
       PB V.

Pearl Bryan V

1910. (Dated by informant). *WKFA*: Notes furnished by D. K.
       Wilgus from W. C. Herd's *Comic and Sentimental Songs*, a
       pocket songster bought by an informant in Kentucky. 12v. &
       chorus, PB V.
1917. Sharp MSS: Mrs. Leona Melton, Macintosh Creek, Hyden,
       Ky. Text 4106. 1v. PB V.
1917. Sharp MSS: Mrs. Poff, Barbourville, Ky. Text 3828. 1v.
       PB V.

1929. Wilson, "Pearl": Miss Clara Moore, Montrose, W.Va. 9v. PB V (includes "album" verse).

1930. Henry, *FSSH*: Miss Rachel Tucker, Varnell, Ga. [Same text given in Henry, "Still More."] 16v. PB V (includes "album" verse).

1930? Scarborough MSS: Gilbert Tallant, Asheville, N.C. 14v. PB V.

1932. (Dated by informant). Collected 1953. *WKFA: Courier-Journal* (Louisville), "Greetings" column, edited by Allan M. Trout, June 29, 1953. Letter from Mrs. Verna Jeffers, Whitley City. 15v. PB V (includes "album" verse).

1935. LC Rec: Bascom Lamar Lunsford, New York. AAFS 1824 B. [Learned from Gilbert Tallant, mentioned above under 1930?] 14v. PB V (includes "album" verse).

1937. LC Rec: Ellie D. Sibert, Clay Co., Ky. AAFS 1477 A. 6v. & chorus, PB V, 1v. unidentified.

1938. LC Rec: Mrs. Pete Steele, Hamilton, Ohio. AAFS 1706 B 2. 9v. PB V.

1938–1939. Hamilton MSS: Anon., Wise Co., Va. 13v. PB V (includes "album" verse).

1939. LC Rec: Mrs. Edith Harmon, Maryville, Tenn. AAFS 2915 B 1. 4v. PB V.

1940. Hamilton MSS: Mrs. Ora Morris, Dungannon, Va. 9v. PB V (includes "album" verse).

pre-1958. Burt, *AMB*: Max Egly, Davis Co., Utah [native of Indiana]. 3v. PB V.

1965. *ACC*: Doc Hopkins, Los Angeles [native of Kentucky]. 2v. PB V, 1v. unidentified, 3v. PB V.

Mixed Texts of Pearl Bryan V

1931. Gordon MSS: Miss Eula Adkins, Whitley Co., Ky. In Mary Newcomb mss. ½v. PB V, 1½v. PB I.

1935. Brewster, *BSI*: Mrs. Flossie Blythe. Contrib. by Miss Larue Smith and Miss Frances Hunt, Oakland City, Gibson Co. 8v. PB I, 5v. PB V.

1958. Forrest Lewis, Parksville, Ky. From unpublished field recording made by Ed Kahn of Los Angeles, Calif. 1v. PB IV, 2v. "The Band Played On," 2v. PB VI, 1v. unidentified, 2v. PB V.

1964?   *The Phipps Family,* Folkways Records FA 2375. 6v. Dalhart
        PB I, 1v. unidentified, 2v. PB II, 2v. unidentified.
1966.   Burton, *ETC*: Mrs. Mary Coyle [learned from print]. 4v.
        PB I, 2v. PB V, 2v. PB I.
1967.   Rev. Dallas Turner (under pseud. "Nevada Slim"), "Pearl
        Bryon." Rural Rhythm RRNS 166-A. Recomposition from PB
        I, II, V.

Pearl Bryan VI

1913.   (Dated by informant). Collected pre-1943. Henry, "Notes
        1943": Mrs. Maud Clark. Contrib. by Mrs. Frank Newell,
        Leonia, N.J. 12v. & chorus, PB VI.
pre-1951.   *WKFA*: Mrs. Effie Carmack, Atascadero, Calif. 6v. PB.
        VI.
1964.   *WKFA*: Anon., Russell Springs. 6v. PB VI.

Mixed Texts of Pearl Bryan VI

1958.   Forrest Lewis, Parksville, Ky. From unpublished field re-
        cording made by Ed Kahn of Los Angeles, Calif. 1v. PB IV,
        2v. "The Band Played On," 2v. PB VI, 1v. unidentified, 2v.
        PB V.

Unclassifiable Texts

1920.   Cox, *FSS*: Clifford R. Meyers, W.Va. Unidentified couplet.
1924.   Brown, *NCF*: Anon., Southern Methodist University, Texas.
        Text not given.
1935.   Brewster, *BSI*: Mrs. H. E. Griesemer. Contrib. by Mr. Junior
        Griesemer, Oakland City, Gibson Co. Text not given.
1936.   Brewster, *BSI*: Mrs. C. H. Allardin, McLeansboro, Ill. [Song
        learned in Indiana.] Text not given.
1936.   Brewster, *BSI*: Mrs. Earl Underhill. Contrib. by Dr. Claude
        Lomax, Dale, Spencer Co. Text not given.
pre-1957.   Musick, "West Va.": Mrs. Amanda Ellen Eddy, Rives-
        ville. 4v. unique text.
1964.   *WKFA*: Mrs. Cecil Burton. One line, unidentified.
1966.   *ACC*: Richard D. Britton, Portland, Ore. 1v. unidentified.

Non-Traditional Texts

1896.   Chas. A. Kennedy (words and music), "Pearl Bryan's Fate,

Waltz Song and Chorus." Published by Ilsen and Co., Cincinnati, copyright February 19, 1896. [Note that copyright date is 17 days after discovery of Pearl Bryan's body and a month before the first trial began.]

1896.   Add. J. Ressequie, Cincinnati, Ohio, "Pearl Bryan's Fate: or the Crime of a Century." Published by J. C. Groene & Co., Cincinnati, copyright 1896. "The original song as sung by Chas. S. Knight at Heck & Avery's Musee, Cincinnati, O." A copy of this sheet music is in the Western Kentucky Folklore Archive, University of California, Los Angeles.

1897.   *Daily Banner Times* (Greencastle), February 25, 1897, "Pearl of Fort Thomas."

1897.   L. C. Seal, Louisville, "The Tell Tale Shoes," published in the *Evening Post* (Louisville), March 20, 1897.

pre-1964.   James W. Day ("Jilson Setters"), no title. Given in Jean Thomas, *Ballad Makin' in the Mountains of Kentucky.*

1965.   *WKFA*: Jess D. Wilson, McKee. Text copied from the singing of Paul Clayton on the LP record *Folk Song Sampler* (Riverside S-2).

1966.   *ACC*: Mrs. Sadie Stalder, Amanda, Ohio, "Pearl Bryon's Song."

BIBLIOGRAPHY

BOOKS AND ARTICLES

Barry, Phillips. "Fair Florella." *American Speech* 3 (1928): 441–447.

Bowra, C. M. *Heroic Poetry*. London: Macmillan, 1952.

Brewster, Paul. *Ballads and Songs of Indiana*. Indiana University Publications, Folklore Series No. 1. Bloomington, 1940.

Brown, Frank C. *The Frank C. Brown Collection of North Carolina Folklore*. Vol. 2. Edited by H. M. Belden and A. P. Hudson. Durham, N.C.: Duke University Press, 1952.

Burt, Olive Wooley. *American Murder Ballads and Their Stories*. New York: Oxford University Press, 1958.

Cambiaire, Celestin Pierre. *East Tennessee and Western Virginia Mountain Ballads*. London: Mitre Press, 1934.

Campbell, Marie. "Survivals of Old Folk Drama in the Kentucky Mountains." *Journal of American Folklore* 51 (1938): 10–24.

Combs, Josiah. *Folk-Songs of the Southern United States*. Edited by D. K. Wilgus. Austin: University of Texas Press, 1967. (A new edition, in English, of *Folk-Songs du Midi des Etats-Unis* [Paris, 1925].)

Cox, John Harrington. *Folk-Songs of the South*. Hatboro, Pa.: Folklore Associates, 1963. (Reprint of 1939 ed.)

Eddy, Mary O. *Ballads and Songs from Ohio*. Hatboro, Pa.: Folklore Associates, 1964. (Reprint of 1939 ed.)

Finger, Charles J. *Frontier Ballads*. New York: Doubleday, 1927.

Gordon, Robert W. Unpublished mss. at the Library of Congress, Washington, D.C.

Henry, Mellinger E. *Folk-Songs from the Southern Highlands*. New York: J. J. Augustin, 1938.

————. "Notes and Queries." *Journal of American Folklore* 42 (1929): 301–303.

————. "Notes and Queries." *Journal of American Folklore* 56 (1943): 139–140.

————. "Still More Ballads and Folk-Songs from the Southern Highlands." *Journal of American Folklore* 45 (1932): 1–176.

Kentucky Reports: Reports of Civil and Criminal Cases Decided by the Court of Appeals of Kentucky. Vol. 100. Louisville: Geo. G. Fetter Printing Co., 1898.

Laws, G. Malcolm. *Native American Balladry*. Rev. ed. Philadelphia: The American Folklore Society, 1964.

Lord, Albert B. *The Singer of Tales*. Cambridge: Harvard University Press, 1960.

Morris, A. C. *Folksongs of Florida*. Gainesville: University of Florida Press, 1950.

Neely, Charles, and John W. Spargo. *Tales and Songs of Southern Illinois*. Menasha, Wisc.: George Banta Publishing Co., 1938.

O'Dwyer, Tom. "Whispering Wires." *Master Detective*, April 1942, pp. 32–40, 57–58.

Pearl Bryan, or: A Fatal Ending. Cincinnati: Barclay & Co., n.d.

Perrow, E. C. "Songs and Rhymes from the South." *Journal of American Folklore* 28 (1915): 129–190.

Pinkerton, Matthew W. *Murder in All Ages*. Chicago: A. E. Pinkerton & Co., 1898.

Poock, L. D. *Headless, Yet Identified; A Story of the Solution of the Pearl Bryan or Fort Thomas Mystery, Through the Shoes*. Columbus: Hann & Adair, Printers, 1897.

Randolph, Vance. *Ozark Folksongs*. Columbia, Mo.: State Historical Society of Missouri, 1945–1950.

————, and Mary Kennedy McCord. "Ozark Friendship Verses." *Journal of American Folklore* 61 (1948): 182–193.

Scarborough, Dorothy. *A Song-Catcher in the Southern Mountains*. New York: Columbia University Press, 1937.

————. Unpublished mss. at Baylor University, Waco, Texas.

Thomas, Jean. *Ballad Makin' in the Mountains of Kentucky*. New York: Oak Publications, 1964. (Reprint of 1939 ed.)

Williams, Cratis. "Ballads and Songs." Master's thesis, University of Kentucky, 1937.

Wilson, Ann Scott. "Pearl Bryan." *Southern Folklore Quarterly* 3 (1939): 15–19.

NEWSPAPERS

Cincinnati Post (Cincinnati, Ohio), April 26–May 7, 1930; February 3, 1946.

Courier-Journal (Louisville, Kentucky), "Greetings" column, edited by Allan M. Trout, June 9–10, 16, 29, 1953; April 3, 5, 1965.

Daily Banner Times (Greencastle, Indiana), February 1, 1896–March 21, 1897.

Enquirer (Cincinnati, Ohio), February 1, 1896–March 21, 1897.

Evening Democrat (Greencastle, Indiana), February 1, 1896–March 21, 1897.

Evening Post (Louisville, Kentucky), February 1, 1896–March 21, 1897.

Greencastle Banner Times (Greencastle, Indiana), February 1, 1896–March 21, 1897.

Greencastle Democrat (Greencastle, Indiana), February 1, 1896–March 21, 1897.

Plain Dealer (Cleveland, Ohio), February 1, 1896–March 21, 1897.

Star-Press (Greencastle, Indiana), February 1, 1896–March 21, 1897.